PLEASE DON'T DIE¿

Rhonda Fried BC,APN,MS,RN

Let's talk about suicide.

About the cover art and artist:

Carmen Martin (**lovelythomas.com**) is a Spanish painter and illustrator living and working in Illinois. Mainly a children's book illustrator, her latest, more personal project explores the power of different emotional states and mood as well as the stigma of mental illness. Her latest series of monochromatic drawings experiment with art as an exercise of mindfulness and a catalyst tool to express those hidden emotions that often stay below the surface.

; The semi-colon is a symbol of suicide interrupted and survival.

Once upon a time, there was an old man who used to go to the ocean to do his writing. He had a habit of walking on the beach every morning before he began his work. Early one morning, he was walking along the shore after a big storm had passed and found the vast beach littered with starfish as far as the eye could see, stretching in both directions.

Off in the distance, the old man noticed a small boy approaching. As the boy walked, he paused every so often and as he grew closer, the man could see that he was occasionally bending down to pick up an object and throw it into the sea. The boy came closer still and the man called out, "Good morning! May I ask what it is that you are doing?"

The young boy paused, looked up, and replied "Throwing starfish into the ocean. The tide has washed them up onto the beach and they can't return to the sea by themselves," the youth replied. "When the sun gets high, they will die, unless I throw them back into the water."

The old man replied, "But there must be tens of thousands of starfish on this beach. I'm afraid you won't really be able to make much of a difference.

The boy bent down, picked up yet another starfish and threw it as far as he could into the ocean. Then he turned, smiled and said, "It made a difference to that one!"

Adapted from *The Star Thrower*, by Loren Eiseley (1907– 1977)

"Find people who can handle your darkest truths, who don't change the subject when you share your pain, or try to make you feel bad for feeling bad. Find people who understand we all struggle, some of us more than others, and that there is no weakness in admitting it. Find people who want to be real, however that looks and feels, and who want you to be real too. Find people who get that life is hard, and who get that life is also beautiful, and who aren't afraid to honor both of these realities. Find people who help you feel more at home in your heart, mind, and body, and who take joy in your joy. Find people who love you, for real, and who accept you, for real. Just as you are. They are out there, these people. Your tribe is waiting for you. Don't stop searching until you find them."

-Scott Stabile, Author of "BIG LOVE"

"Jumper" by Third Eye Blind

I wish you would step back from that ledge my friend,

You could cut ties with all the lies, that you've been living in,

And if you do not want to see me again, I would understand. I would understand,

The angry boy, a bit too insane, Icing over a secret pain,

You know you don't belong,

You're the first to fight, You're way too loud, You're the flash of light, On a burial shroud,

I know something's wrong,

Well everyone I know has got a reason, To say, put the past away, I wish you would step back from that ledge my friend,

You could cut ties with all the lies, That you've been living in,

And if you do not want to see me again, I would understand, I would understand.

Well he's on the table, And he's gone to code, And I do not think anyone knows,

What they are doing here,

And your friends have left, You've been dismissed,

I never thought it would come to this, And I, I want you to know, Everyone's got to face down the demons,

Maybe today, We can put the past away,

I wish you would step back from that ledge my friend,

You could cut ties with all the lies, that you've been living in,

And if you do not want to see me again, I would understand, I would understand,

I would understand...

Can you put the past away, I wish you would step back from that ledge my friend, I would understand.

Songwriters: Stephan Jenkins; Jumper lyrics © BMG Rights Management US, LLC

"Flames' by David Guetta & Sia

Oh, oh

One foot in front of the other babe One breath leads to another yeah Just keep moving, oh

Look within for the strength today Listen out for the voice to say

Just keep moving, oh

Go, go, go

Figure it out, figure it out, but don't stop moving Go, go, go

Figure it out, figure it out, you can do this

So my love, keep on running

You gotta get through today, yeah There my love, keep on running Gotta keep those tears at bay, oh Oh, my love, don't stop burning Gonna send them up in flames

In flames

Don't stop, tomorrow's another day Don't stop, tomorrow you'll feel no pain Just keep moving, oh

Don't stop the past'll trip you up

You know, right now's gotta be enough Just keep moving

Go, go, go

Figure it out, figure it out, but don't stop moving Go, go, go

Figure it out, figure it out, you can do this

Songwriters: Sia Furler, David Guetta, Christopher Braide, Giorgio Tuinfort, Marcus van Wattum; ©What A Music 2018

Verses from "The Middle" by Jimmy Eat World
Hey
Don't write yourself off yet
It's only in your head you feel left out or looked down on Just
do your best
Do everything you can
Don't you worry what their bitter hearts are going to say
It just takes some time
Little girl, you're in the middle of the ride Everything,
everything will be just fine Everything, everything will be all
right

...

Dedication

This book is dedicated to the late Dr. R. Traisman, who saved me from myself; to my grandmother Milly, who made me feel truly loved for the first time in my life as a child; to my family especially my wonderful husband Rich who has always been supportive of all my crazy ideas; to my patients past and present whom I have learned from and taught me to be a better listener; and to all those whose lives were ever touched by suicide. Thank you to my cousins Kotch and David for sharing their experiences over the years, after Tamara ended her life.

This book is published with great thanks to the survivors who work to stay alive and work to heal; who in many ways contributed to this book; and with special gratefulness to the family of Laura, who shared her journals to help us see inside the mind of someone preparing to leave this earth.

This book is especially for you, if you've ever thought o f killing yourself or know someone who has. You are not alone. Many of us struggle with depression, loss and feeling that we don't fit in. You are not alone. It's okay to be different. You can survive pain. You can overcome failure. If you just hang in there, you can get through this. You are not alone.

"There are only two days in the year that nothing can be done. One is called Yesterday and the other is called Tomorrow. Today is the right day to Love, Believe, Do and mostly, Live."

Dalai Lama XIV

NEED IMMEDIATE HELP?

National Suicide Prevention Lifeline
1 (800) 273-8255

Hours: 24 hours, 7 days a week
Languages: English, Spanish
Website: www.suicidepreventionlifeline.org

TABLE OF CONTENTS

"But what about all those warnings about taking those medications? They can cause people to have suicidal thoughts who didn't have them before? How can medication be a good idea if one of the risks of antidepressants is that it can worsen suicidal thoughts? What's the point of taking a medicine that can make me feel worse? " p.76

"Isn't suicide a sin?" p.81

"Most people who kill themselves have a mental illness" p.82

Chapter 3. Suicide Prevention p.84

Chapter 4. Suicide Prevention: Teaching Coping and Self Calming Strategies p.108

Chapter 5. Suicide Survival: Recovery, Forgiveness and Shame p. 172

Chapter 6. Case studies and Discussion p. 178

Conclusion p.202

Acknowledgment p.203

Resources and References p.204

Introduction

My story: Let's Talk about Suicide

Like many who work in mental health, I've come to this path after a lifelong struggle with my own demons. I've mostly recovered from Major Depression with the help of medication and vitamins, because anyone who's experienced knows it's always a process. At 11 years old, I wanted to die. At 13, I made my first suicide attempt. I live with ADD. It's been challenging and I've worked hard, but I've recovered. I've recovered from being a person who hated myself and made poor life choices to one who helps others. Those others wanted a provider who truly understood their pain. I wouldn't be here to help them know without a lot of work to get better.

I survived with the help of a wonderful therapist, and I continue to strive to be my best self. I still read every self- help book that I think will help myself or my patients. I've taken the best from those books, applied the Science, and reached a very good place mentally. I work in a successful outpatient psychiatric practice which I enjoy very much. This is my second book. The first was a self -help book titled "True Love; Breaking the Cycle of Failed Relationships" based on a plan I devised to clean up my personal life and choices. I would like to help others navigate these challenges. I've persevered through many personal hardships and I've flourished in spite of numerous personal imperfections.

I would like to help others navigate and survive depression, and hopefully, feel grounded and flourish, as well. This was the whole reason I chose this career.

Why did I survive when others who tried what I did -did not? I don't have that answer.

I started writing this book in 2014, but found it so painful, I started to believe that I could not get it finished. Yet, I had made a promise to myself, and to Tamara's and Laura's family that I would. Telling the story of survival from the perspective of both the patient and the provider might help others in a different way. Ultimately, it was the voices of those who left us too soon, that seemed to shout to me, get this done! I could not silence them, so I wrote.

When I was a child, I did not feel particularly gifted in any way, nor particularly attractive, wanted or loved. I felt that I lived in the shadow of my brother and sister. My father worked too much and was usually short-tempered when he was around. His expectations of his children were to "be seen and not heard." Later in life, he explained he did what his father did to him.

My mother was hardly prepared to be a parent, although she followed the script written out for her by society at the time. Be pretty, marry well, have children. No one talked then about what to do with them once you had them and she certainly didn't know. My mother became fatherless when she was 3 during the Great Depression. She mostly entertained herself in her crib while my grandmother worked 20 hour days, until her older sister came home from school (Helen was 11) and took care of her.

My mother grew up in a time where marriage was a way to be taken care of, and if you were attractive enough, you picked the best option whom you thought would take the best care of you. I don't think she knew or thought there were any other options.

My older brother seemed to be very close with my father, compared to myself. He was groomed to follow in dad's family business. My younger sister was my mother's pride and joy, she was probably most like my mother in that she was very pretty and petite. I was loud, I couldn't sit still or shut up. ADD wasn't something people thought about back then, and when it was considered, it was thought to be something boys had, not girls.

My first vivid memory was age 3 when my mother brought my new sister home from the hospital. All the relatives were over, lots of people, to meet this new baby. My mother looked very happy showing her off. I remember this day as the first time I truly felt invisible. For a brief period, I rebelled against this invisibility. I held my breath at the top of the stairs of the three story apartment building where we lived, until I passed out and tumbled down the stairs. My mother knew something was amiss so she asked the pediatrician for advice. The advice she was given was to ignore me, so after that I tumbled down the steps a few more times and eventually I stopped.

Feeling as invisible as I did, I began to hide in dark closets to see how many hours it would take for anyone to notice I wasn't around. I spent hours there and often cried myself to sleep. No one noticed until mealtime. I waited until I heard my name called out a few times before I sullenly came to the table for dinner, where we also were to be seen and not heard.

3

I did have one special person who I looked forward to being with, my father's mother. Having had no daughters, Milly spent as much time with me as possible. I basked in her attention. I was fortunate to have spent two weekends every month with her, and there, I always felt special. I fantasized that she was my real mother. It was a respite from all the sadness, and Milly spoiled me, was proud of me, and regaled me with future trips we would take together one day. Until Milly left on vacation and never returned. I was 11 and felt my whole world ended when she died. I lost the only adult I knew loved me and wanted to be with me.

When she died, I knew I was truly alone. It felt as though the earth stopped and all love stopped that day. I experienced my first major depression which lasted until I was about 30 years old.

At 13, I had my first boyfriend, and "went steady" for a while, and I started feeling special again, even when away for camp for the summer. Then the boy broke up with me to be with his old girlfriend while I was gone.

Prior to leaving, Twiggy became the new modeling sensation, making unobtainable thinness the body goal for girls. I discovered how to finally control my chubbiness for the first time in my life by stopping eating. I became very thin and received lots of attention for this as well. When the compliments stopped, I just tried to get thinner. After receiving the

boyfriend break up letter, I began binging.

Then, upon my return from camp, I swallowed an

4

entire bottle of aspirin, and other miscellaneous pills in the medicine cabinet-over 200 pills. I laid down to die, relieved to be rid of my misery. My pain felt immense and intolerable. No one loved me, and I was old enough to figure out what to do about it. It was devastating to me that I woke up. I felt so angry but then was so sick I couldn't think of anything else but obeying my body. No one ever knew what happened. Everyone just thought I had the flu. After a few days, my body healed itself. If I had died that day, my family would have had very little idea why.

What is the difference between that scenario and Laura's, a beautiful young lady we'll discuss in the case studies in Chapter 5? Random luck. Sometimes, the people who survive a suicide attempt realize in a later point in their life, that they were just lucky. Nowadays, we are more educated about such things, and hopefully today someone would have given my mother more helpful advice. Perhaps as a teen, I might have even reached out to someone for help or someone might have reached out to me. My life began really changing after reading Dr. David Burns' book "Feeling Good; The New Mood Therapy" which instructed me in how to change my thought processes. I practiced and practiced, and it worked.

How can we encourage people who are overcome with despair choose life? We can only do this with people who admit the level of despair they are in, and by educating all of us to reach out to others who seem depressed and isolated. The whole concept of stigma and shame about mental health is absurd. We would

never judge someone with diabetes or blindness and think they caused their own illness. Why do we still do this with mental health?

Perhaps we can reduce the number of people who feel so hopeless if we can take suicide out of the closet and start talking about it instead.

Depression is not a character flaw. It is not a sign of weakness; it is a medical condition and a very serious one. There is much we can do to help those who are suffering. While we can't prevent all suicides, we can prevent some, and even one is worthwhile.

Every suicide affects many other lives; it is estimated by the CDC that each suicide deeply affects at least 6 other people. What can we do to help those who are suffering? Can we prevent some suicides from occurring? What can we learn from those we have lost? Learning, talking, and discussing suicide could save someone's life. If I save someone, and you save someone, we've really made an impact on this earth, don't you think? What could be more important?

When I was first treated, there was a lot of stigma about mental health and medications, which remains today. Recent scientific breakthroughs suggest that science will eventually disprove the notion that depression or anxiety is "just in your head" and we will come to regard mental illness as physical and measurable like every other medical condition. Just because Plato couldn't prove the world was round, didn't mean his theory about it was wrong. The technology to understand the brain and mental illness are still very much in their infancy. For this reason, this book will contain lots of information. Some of it is based on my personal experience of chronic depression and survival of multiple suicide attempts. Some of it is based on my clinical experience in

working with others dealing with a lot of issues that
made them feel death was a better choice than life.
Some of the information is from working with
survivors whose family members choose suicide.
Some is based on science, and some is based on other
experts and epidemiology studies. Because the
science of psychiatry is still in its infancy, right now
we don't know why some people think all the time
about ending their lives and some people are lucky
enough never to have that thought ever cross their
minds.

Some genetic link will be identified, just as genetics
identifying who is predisposed to cancer and other
diseases are being discovered. The first genetic issue
that influences predisposition to depression and
anxiety has already been identified. Those at high risk
of developing depression and anxiety because of
issues with absorbing L-methylfolate, a substance
needed by the brain to produce the needed
neurochemicals to make serotonin, has already been
discovered and is already influencing current
treatment.

Here I must share that along with many of my
patients, the prescription of L methylfolate called
Deplin changed my life. My medications worked
significantly better and suicidal thoughts no longer
became the first thing I thought of when I felt
overwhelmed.

A second genetic factor that has already been
identified which is the type of allele you have. Alleles

are transporter genes for serotonin and there has been
found to be different lengths. These different types
and lengths of this transporter gene have been

7

determined to affect how resilient you are too stressful life circumstances. Your allele type can already be identified on a simple genetic test performed using a cheek swab at a providers office. This science is still very young, but certain transport types are thought to lead to increased issues which predispose some to depression and PTSD. I have no doubt there will be many more genetic factors identified, including one for who is predisposed to suicide.

Mental illness and depression distort your view of reality. I continued to deal with depression for many years after I started working with others. People can walk around every day feeling depressed and because this is so familiar, they don't even realize it's possible to feel differently. Then something terrible can happen, and the balance of existing painfully just becomes too much to bear.

Suicide isn't always preventable. But there are a lot of things we can do, and learn to help prevent as many as possible and just like the Star Thrower story about theboy throwing the starfish back into the ocean and the old man saying, 'Why bother, there are thousands of starfish washed up on this beach, and the boy answering it will make a difference to this one', I'm hoping to make a difference for one.

When I first started writing this book in 2014, I wanted it to be as thorough and comprehensive as possible. Since then, the attention to suicide has grown tremendously and I am glad to see this. I've

taken a step back from my completely comprehensive goal in favor of finishing this work knowing that we will continue to learn much, but I think I've included the most current and important research and modalities for treatment and interventions as of 2018. It is time for me to finish this book.

This is a sad book about a painful topic, and might be as hard to read as it was to write. Read what is useful to you. Put it down if it makes you too sad. Take care of yourself and get help if you need it. If the help you find is not what you need, look elsewhere. It's out there, I promise.

Sources:
Feeling Good; The New Mood Therapy by Dr David Burns MD

"The genetics of mental illness: implications for practice", Dr. Steven E. Hyman. Bulletin of the World Health Organization, 2000, 78 (4)

"Serotonin Transporter Gene as a Predictor of Stress Generation in Depression" Dr Lisa R Starr, Constance

Hammen, Patricia A Brennan, and Jake M Najman. J Abnorm Psychol. 2012 Nov; 121(4): 810–818.
The Star Thrower by Loren Eiseley, 1979

Chapter 1:   Suicide and Risk Factors

Please don't die

Suicide in our country is a serious health crisis. Approximately 46,000 people in the US end their lives each year, and because of under-reporting, the real number is possibly twice as high. It's the 10th leading cause of death in the United States according to the CDC 2018 report, having moved up from #11 in the last few years, and the rates continue to rise. When the media reports that approximately 22 veterans of the armed services take their own lives daily, it is a big issue. When a teen suicides, and following this a string of suicides at school follow, it's tragic. When a celebrity dies by their own hand, it affects many. The recent CDC reports the majority of those who die by suicide as having no known mental illness. The most common contributing factors were relationship issues, life stressors, recent or impending crises, physical health problems and substance abuse. The leading contributing factor to suicide around the world is having a terminal illness. In this Chapter, we will explore incidence and contributing factors around the world, as well as populations at greatest risk in the US. In Chapter 5 we will explore some real life examples of people who have died by suicide and identify the stressors and risk factors that preceded their actions in an attempt to better understand their reasons. We'll begin by exploring suicide rates around the world and some of the reasons why those countries' rates are so high.

International Suicide Rates

Country	Men (%)	Women (%)	Total Population (% per 100, 000 people)
Guyana	70.80	22.1	44.2
Democratic People's of Korea	45.4	35.1	38.5
South Korea	41.7	18.0	28.9
Sri Lanka	46.5	12.8	28.8
Lithuania	51.0	8.4	28.2
Japan	18.5	10.1	26.9
Poland	16.6	3.8	30.5
Belgium	7.7	21.0	20.0
Finland	7.5	22.2	14.8
France	6.0	12.3	19.3
Austria	5.4	11.5	18.2
United States	5.2	11.1	19.4
United Kingdom	2.6	6.2	9.8

Source: World Population Review; World Health Organization

Suicide is an issue in the U.S., but of course happens everywhere. The reasons people take their own lives, and who choose their own death vary from country to country.

For example, South Korea is an advanced industrialized nation, but they are third in the world in their incidence of death by suicide. In that country, the highest risk group are senior citizens. Traditionally seniors lived in extended families with their children, but families no longer live this way. Traditionally, when a parent aged, that parent or elder relative was cared for in the home by the rest of the family. This aspect of their civilization changed along with the increased mobility of families seen in all industrialized nations, but occurred without the public programs like subsidized housing, nursing homes, assisted living buildings and Medicare we enjoy in the US. As seniors felt displaced and faced financial stressors along with the decline in health that accompanies aging, some turned to suicide to end their lives so as not to be a burden to their families.

South Korea's suicide rate and the age of those who are most likely to suicide reflects the economic stress and social changes in that country. Seniors have lost the feeling of being useful and needed, an important aspect to one's self esteem. They are socially isolated, financially stressed and struggling physically. Suicide seems a viable choice.

Contrast South Korea with the country with the highest suicide rate, Guyana. Guyana has more in common with other impoverished countries where suicide is more prevalent such as Sri Lanka (#4). In these countries, finances and poverty contribute, and women have dependent roles with few or no options if

12

their male relatives or spouses are abusive. Younger women have higher suicide numbers compared to industrialized nations where mental health care is available. There are negative stigmas about mental illness and fewer choices about reproductive rights. The majority of the women who commit suicide are under 18 years old.

An additional contributing factor in impoverished countries has to do with HIV incidence. HIV feels like a death sentence, and getting a diagnosis of HIV when one can see the impacts it has on health over time can be overwhelming. There is also social stigma connected to HIV. While HIV still increases the incidence of having suicidal ideation in developed nations, the support systems as well as role models of people living long and productive lives in developed countries can offset that initial despair versus the outcomes expected in countries with poverty, poor health care access and little to no emotional or physical support.

Shame is another a factor that affects a decision to suicide. Shame is more prevalent in some cultures than others. In Japan, the suicide rate has reached 70 people a day. Men in Japan are significantly more likely to suicide than women, and suicide there is often related to job loss or economic failure, but is also high during divorce. Suicide has less of a taboo in Japan than it has in the U.S., where most religions consider it a sin. In our country, it is shameful to commit suicide because it violates religious beliefs. Japan's culture is not based on Judeo-Christian beliefs. In Japan's history, suicide was regarded at as heroic and an accepted way to restore family honor. During World War II, kamikaze pilots used their planes as weapons, killing themselves in the process of attacking others. These pilots were considered heroes.

This concept of honor dates as far back as the Samurai warriors finding honor in suicide for failing their masters, or themselves. Today, too, senior Japanese may choose to kill themselves in order to provide for their extended families. Suicides are rarely investigated in Japan and life insurance policies are silent on suicide as a reason not to pay out benefits. In addition, cremation after death is much more common, which eliminates most evidence of suicide quickly.

Suicide in Japan is also growing very quickly for younger men as well. Japan's society is more rule based and rigid, allowing for less diversity. People are expected to keep their fears and feelings contained. There is still a great social taboo on mental illness. People have very little understanding of depression. This along with less occupational security since the financial crisis of the last 20 years there result in more Japanese feeling they can't handle the expectations of their families. Young men not able to meet their families' expectations can consider suicide an honorable choice. In addition, there is increased social isolation as technology replaces social interactions. This is a risk factor in many industrialized nations as well. In the upcoming Chapter 4, in the section on Happiness, we'll talk about the recent study of increased social isolation in our country related to technology and how this has increased depression incidence here.

Suicide in the United States

The 2018 CDC report states that the rate of suicide in our country rose 25% from 1999 to 2016, which amounts to approximately 121 suicides per day. For every suicide completion, 12-25 people attempt it. Suicide rates have been rising steadily in almost every state.

Nevada, North Dakota, and Vermont saw increases topping 50%. In the US, depression- a high risk factor for suicide, is also on the rise.

Each year, close to 500,000 people visit a hospital for injuries due to self-harm. Because of the way this data is collected, we are not able to distinguish intentional suicide attempts from non-intentional self-harm behaviors, but the medical cost is high. The estimated cost of these hospital visits in the U.S. is 44 billion dollars annually.

Many suicide attempts go unreported or untreated. Surveys suggest that at least one million people in the U.S. each year engage in intentionally inflicted self-harm. In 2015, the highest suicide rate (19.6 deaths daily) was among adults between 45 and 64 years of age. The second highest rate (19.4) occurred in those 85 years or older. Younger groups have had consistently lower suicide rates than middle-aged and older adults. In 2015, adolescents and young adults aged 15 to 24 had a daily suicide rate of 12.5.

In 2015, the highest U.S. suicide rate (15.1 deaths daily) was among Whites and the second highest rate (12.6) was among American Indians and Alaska Natives. White males accounted for 7 out of 10 suicides in 2015. Much lower and roughly similar rates were found among Hispanics (5.8), Asians and Pacific Islanders (6.4), and Blacks (5.6).

Females attempt suicide three times more often than males. As with suicide deaths, rates of attempted suicide vary considerably among demographic groups. While males are 4 times more likely than females to die by suicide, females attempt suicide 3 times as often as males. The ratio of suicide attempts to suicide death in youth is estimated to be about 25:1, compared to about 4:1 in the elderly. Suicide attempts were once thought of to be a 'cry for help', but research has shown that suicide attempts are a high predictor of who may successfully end their own lives at a later point in time. Likely due to the high prevalence and availability of guns in the US, firearms are involved in almost 50% of all suicides here.

High Risk Groups:
Children and Teens

Teen suicide is a growing health concern. According to 2018 CDC statistics, suicide is the second leading cause of death for those under 10 years old in the US. In a 2018 study by Plemmons, the rate of hospital ER visits continues to rise for children between ages 5-17, with the highest incidence among teens. The highest incidence occurs in October, shortly after the pressures of school kicks in as school creates both performance and social stress. Children with mental health issues are happier over the summer with no pressures.
Suicide is the third-leading cause of death for young people ages 15 to 24. One in five teenagers in the

U.S. seriously considers suicide annually, according to data collected by the CDC. In 2003, 8 percent of adolescents attempted suicide, representing approximately 1 million teenagers, of whom nearly 300,000 received medical attention for their attempt. Approximately 1,700 teenagers die by suicide each year. Currently, the most effective suicide prevention programs equip mental health professionals and other community educators and leaders with sufficient resources to recognize who is at risk and who has access to mental health care. There seems to be a phenomenon of copycat suicides that often occur in clusters in school environments requiring special attention and specific interventions by the community and school.

A recent study focused on the effectiveness of early childhood intervention in children with depression. The study showed the effectiveness of psychotherapy modules which included the parents, in young children. The group was compared to a group of children on the waiting list for the program, using standardized assessment tools to compare the outcomes and mental states of the two groups. The group who experienced early intervention psychotherapy with their parents demonstrated improvement in their depression. They were involved in 20 weeks of psychotherapeutic interventions with specific modules to address depression and emotional regulation. They improved significantly and many went into remission. Meanwhile, not only did the control group not improve, they also developed co-morbid anxiety. (*16). Their intervention did not involve medications. The groups will be followed long term going forward to see if their depression returned at some later point in life. It would be wonderful if depression could be treated early, so that more serious problems didn't occur later as teens. "Many parents, not to speak of psychiatrists and other physicians, are wary about prescribing antidepressants to teenagers after the FDA issued a "black box" warning, in 2004, that use of SSRI antidepressant medications was linked to an increased risk of suicidal thoughts or behaviors.

The FDA based its warning on a review of records of nearly 2,200 children treated with SSRI medications, finding that 4 percent experienced suicidal thinking or behavior - twice the rate of those taking placebos. There were no completed suicides among the 2,200 children treated.

Three years later a comprehensive review of pediatric trials, funded by the National Institute of Mental Health and conducted between 1988 and 2006, found that the benefits of these medications likely outweigh their risks to children and adolescents with serious depression and anxiety.

And after the warning was in place, the Centers for Disease Control and Prevention reported not a decrease but a sharp *increase* in the suicide rate for 10- to 19- year-olds. This dramatic increase coincided with a drop in antidepressant prescriptions for teens.

.

> Untreated depression can be lethal to adolescents. For many, medication is a lifeline.
>
> -Harold S. Koplewicz, MD

In the following excerpt, Dr. Christopher Johnson, President of Pediatric Intensive Care Associates, P.C., as Medical Director of the PICU for CentraCare Health Systems shared some of his thoughts on his blog chrisjohnsonmd.com:

> *"After years of declining, the suicide rate in our country has been increasing, now at about 125% of the rate of several decades ago. This increase accelerated after 2006. Although all age groups showed an increase, the rate among women, particularly adolescent girls, took a notable jump. In 2012 suicide was the second leading cause of death in*

adolescents ages 12 to 19 years, accounting for more deaths in this age group than cancer, heart disease, influenza, pneumonia, diabetes mellitus, human immunodeficiency virus, and stroke combined. Here are some recent statistics of women from the CDC, although they don't quite break out adolescents the way I would like.

Actual suicide is just the tip of the iceberg, since, at least among adolescent girls who attempt it, typically, with a drug overdose, there are as many as 90 attempts for every death. Since a large number of these attempts end up in the PICU, I'm not surprised we are seeing more and more of them come through our doors. A few other points are worth noting here. The success statistics for adolescent boys are unfortunately much higher because boys tend to use more violent means than girls, such as hanging, firearms, or automobiles. Although rates for boys are up slightly, they really haven't changed much. It's also important to realize suicide attempts are a spectrum -- some are more serious than others. Many girls take an overdose and then immediately tell somebody about it. These are often called suicide gestures and can be quite impulsive

They may leave a suicide note. I couldn't find any data about whether these different categories are discordant in the rate increase, but I assume the two are tracking

*togeher. Finally, a child may not know
which drugs are truly dangerous. I have
seen very serious suicide attempts by
children who take overdoses of what we
know to be innocuous medications, but the
child does not. Regardless of what
category the attempt is, of course, the child
needs mental health services subsequently.
These days we find a child's text messages
to be very helpful.*

*So why the increase in adolescent girls?
Presumably, suicide rates are rough and
ready markers for rates of depression. Is
teen depression increasing? A 2006 study
says no, at least up until then. What about
the last decade, since 2006 appears to be
the year suicide rates inflected upward in
adolescent girls. I did find a snapshot for
2015 from the CDC of the number of
adolescents who experienced a major
depressive episode during the year -- girls
were nearly 20%. A recent study in
Pediatrics, the journal of the American
Academy of Pediatrics, found a nearly
50% increase in adolescent depression
over the past 11 years. Mental health
problems are notoriously difficult to study
because, of course, we have no definitive
test for them -- no blood test, no fancy
brain scans. We mostly rely on surveys.
Still, it does seem something changed
about a decade ago, and this is probably
reflected in the increase in suicide attempts
among girls at roughly the same rate as
the increase in major depression.*

There are a few other things to keep in mind.

Prescriptions of antidepressants have increased dramatically, particularly of drugs in the class we call selective serotonin re-uptake inhibitors (SSRIs). Common brand names for these are Prozac, Paxil, Celexa, and Zoloft. There has been concern that in the short term after starting them, SSRIs may actually increase thoughts about suicide in adolescents. Another new development is social media. Teenagers, especially those in difficult home situations or who are socially isolated, are quite susceptible to bullying behavior, and cyberbullying has emerged as a new threat to such children. There have been several dramatic cases in the news about suicides following cyberbullying.

"I'm sorry to say I really don't know what explains these increasing rates, except to point out the overall rate of suicide for the whole population has also increased to some extent; it was 10.5 deaths per 100,000 persons in 1999 and is now 13 per 100,000. Middle-aged males have seen a dramatic jump in rates. It appears to me that, for many possible reasons, there is more social anxiety and depression in America, which in turn increases suicide rates. Adolescent girls are feeling this in particular. You might say our entire society is issuing a cry for help.

Christopher Johnson, MD, is a pediatric intensive care physician, and author of Keeping Your Kids Out of the Emergency Room: A Guide to Childhood Injuries and Illnesses, Your Critically Ill Child: Life and Death Choices Parents Must Face, How to Talk to Your Child's Doctor: A Handbook for Parents, and How Your Child Heals: An Inside Look At Common Childhood Ailments. He blogs at his self-titled site, Christopher Johnson, MD. This post appeared on KevinMD.com

According to the Department of Health and Human Services,("HHS") between 2010 and 2016 the number of adolescents who experienced a "Major Depressive Episode" grew by 60% . In 2016, HHS performed a nationwide poll of 17,000 teens and found that at least 13% of them had experienced a major depressive episode the previous year, compared with an 8% frequency for the same poll conducted in 2010. The rates of suicide deaths has risen continuously and has reached a 40 year high, according to the CDC. This is in contrast to the late 1990s and early 2000s when rates held steady or declined.

Dr. Jean Twenge of San Diego State University surveyed 500,000 teens nationwide and felt there might be a link between technology usage and mood. The more time adolescents spent on their smartphones, the more depressed they seemed to be. There is some suggestion that the low resulting face time contact between young people could be contributing to depressed mood, but it is also possible that depressed teens tend to isolate more and occupy themselves with technology rather than people and activities.

This social isolation can worsen self-esteem issues already present. Kids and adults tend to bully more on social media platforms, because it's much easier to be cruel to someone when you don't see the reaction it makes on the receiver. Even lack of "likes" to postings on social media setting may be interpreted as failure or rejection. So it is not that surprising that there is some correlation between the two factors. Two hours or more daily spent on smart phone appears connected to increased incidence of depression.

As a parent, the scariest thing to live with is the fear of anything bad happening to our child. I understand the fear, but it is just as harmful to let our children avoid all of life's challenges. Parents are so afraid of suicide risk, that they sometimes enable the teens to manipulate into school avoidance, refuse therapy and refuse the medications and treatments that are necessary to help them. I see more and more cases of teens unlikely to successfully launch into adulthood. Teens have to learn to navigate failure and disappointment, and this has to be taught at home. We want to protect our children but there is such a thing as protecting too much. It can be a challenge and parents should seek out psychological assistance early to help with this process when they see signs that frighten them.

When young people take their own lives, this often becomes a public suicide, because they've usually done it for reasons that don't make sense to adults, in an environment where so many people are touched by it. It affects everyone in their classes at school who tell their parents and friends. It becomes news and can trigger copycat suicides. When you're young, you have the same intensity of pain from the losses and disappointments in your life without the same ability to put them in perspective and cope with those feelings. It is a particularly vulnerable and difficult time. Young people, just embarking on the complicated emotions that adulthood brings can easily become overwhelmed and make impulsive decisions. While there remain many things we do not know about the human brain, we do know that the positives of using medications when a person is depressed far outweigh the risks.

These types of medications have been around for over 35 years now with few if any, life threatening or shortening consequences. On the flip side, the decisions one can make when trying to function when seriously depressed most definitely have life threatening consequences. The statistics of those who are adolescent who do commit suicide are much stronger in those who are not taking an antidepressant or not in treatment. When young people take their lives, they do it when they're not getting help, because if they are engaged in treatment, they have someone to tell when they are struggling. When teens commit suicide, they are usually not in, or have dropped out of treatment.

Finding the right medication and therapy can be a frustrating process that takes a lot of time, patience, and support. Parents are sometimes too fearful to help the teen navigate this process to its completion. Both are often needed to navigate to successful resolution of emotional issues.

Health insurance for mental health is very expensive,and mental health coverage may be limited, causing another barrier to access care and treatment.

25

Insurance may pay only half of the cost of therapy, making access unaffordable. Or an insurance carrier may pay pennies towards what a usual fee could be, making finding good providers who accept it very difficult. Although it is a frustrating process to find the right treatment, there is a genetic test which helps predict which medications are more likely to cause side effects for each patient. This test can help shorten the trial period to finding a successful treatment.

When the teen hears or senses the parent complaining about the cost, or about the time it takes to bring them to treatment, this becomes another issue the teen feels bad about that might affect their interest in participating.

Parents are often overwhelmed by the financial hardship posed by the care. I have seen many situations where the teen truly needed long term residential treatment to address their serious mental health concerns. The parents are fully on board until they learn that insurance doesn't provide the coverage and that the expense involved is equal to four years of college. However, the results have paid for themselves in the differences made by these programs for their child. Even for one young adult patient of mine who signed themselves out when they became of age, this young person is now an insightful productive adult even though the relationship with the parents remains estranged.

Children and teens can make comments when they are upset such as "I wish I was never born", or "I wish I was dead." These comments are opportunities for you as a loved one to talk about those thoughts with them.

You can acknowledge how frustrated they are, but you will hopefully also let them know how important their presence on earth is to you as well, and how much you love them. I would never minimize the impact of making these statements can have later, if you have the opportunity. Sometimes as parents we can put too much emphasis on achievements and behavior.

I do believe that talking is the biggest way we can impact the prevalence of suicide. First we have to start talking about it a lot more in schools, so that when people do have those thoughts, they don't think they're "sick" or abnormal. A desire to run away from pain is programmed in our response to fear; flight, fight, or freeze. The desire to extinguish pain can overtake any other thoughts, when the pain is bad enough. Giving someone the opportunity to talk about that pain is a gift. You don't have to do anything but ask, listen, and let the person know they are important to you. As a nation, we have to do more things to encourage the resilience in our children and ourselves. This will not be a book that only talks about what's wrong and not how to fix it.

We'll discuss how to nurture resilience in children and adults in more detail in Chapter 3.

High Risk Group: Veterans

The suicide rate among veterans has become a public health crisis. In 2016, an average of 20-22 veteran suicides occurred each day. The incidence of mental health issues among veterans has also risen drastically during this period. The US Department of Veteran Affairs created a "call to action" to study and intervene with this population. Comprehensive data analyses were done to identify more information and more access to treatment. Here are some of their conclusions:

In 2014, an average of 20 Veterans died by suicide each day. 6 of the 20 were recent users of VHA services, and in 2017, this number was increased to 22 lives lost daily. In 2014, Veterans accounted for 18% of all deaths by suicide among US adults; veterans account for 8.5% of the US population. This is actually a reduction from 20.1% of suicide deaths by veterans in 2010, because the VA has made the problem an area of focus and devoted numerous resources to help those in need.

67% of Veteran suicides involve firearms. About 65% were age 50 and over. Even after adjusting for age and sex, risk of suicide in veterans is 22% higher than in the civilian population. From 2001 to 2014, as the civilian suicide rate rose about 23.3 percent, the rate of suicide among veterans jumped more than 32 percent. The problem is particularly worrisome among female veterans, who saw their suicide rates rise more than 85 percent over that time, compared to about 40 percent for civilian women.

Prior to 2006, the rates of veteran suicides were lower than the rates in the general population, but these rates began a steady rise since that time. Veterans continue to be one of the highest suicide risk groups, and there are a variety of risk factors that contribute. Being deployed away from one's family can cause disruptions in relationships. Returns can be highly anticipated but disappointing. Training can result in discharged vets being uncomfortable or unable to show or reveal their true feelings with others, since this behavior is discouraged while deployed. If one acknowledges depression during deployment, this is a cause for discharge. One veteran I treat confided that he actually walked toward gunfire when he felt depressed and those around him were being killed, and he wanted to die because he was so miserable. If a deployed or active duty person requests treatment to help them cope with what they might be seeing or feeling, this may be a cause for discharge without benefits unless the condition is considered occupationally caused. Basic training can be experienced as demeaning, lowering self-esteem. Assignments, and failure to reach expected promotions can be discouraging. Deployment can result in injury and dealing with adjusting to civilian life with chronic emotional or physical pain can be very challenging.

These people have access to weapons. These and other factors contribute to make veterans a group with high suicide statistics. Age is also a big factor. Sixty five percent of all veteran suicides in 2014 were for individuals 50 years or older, many of whom spent little or no time fighting in the most recent wars.

All branches of the military have undertaken campaigns to reduce suicides. Providing access now to the Veterans Crisis Line, the Military Crisis Line, DCoE Outreach Center and other resources may reduce the incidence and address this issue. Yet, having a mental illness while in active duty may result in discharge, and therefore, may try to conceal the issue. This creates new challenges in identifying who is at risk. Participation in the military also requires the ability to control emotions and keep secrets. These behaviors will continue throughout life and may reduce the ability to connect intimately and emotionally with others. Add to this the aspects of aging, and the effects aging has on previous injuries both physical and emotional, and this remains a high risk group. Deployment related PTSD is another factor contributing to risk.

The 2016 Office of Veterans affairs also had some positive news. Not every veteran is eligible for VHA services, but among those who received those services, suicide rates were lower. The efforts made to reach out and provide more support have had an impact. The number of veterans who were classified as having a service related disability more than doubled.

Compared to 2001, the rates of suicide have decreased among VHA patients identified with a mental illness. Unfortunately, rates of suicide among VHA patients diagnosed with Opoid Use Disorders have increased over this same time period. The highest rates and most vulnerable periods for veterans occur in the period following separation from Active Duty from a combat deployment.

High Risk Group: Seniors, White Males

According to CDC data, the highest rates of suicide occur among men ages 75 and older. For those who aren't dissuaded by their religious sanctions, aging along with the illness and suffering that go along with this can become unbearable. A 71 year old man recently was just released from the hospital where he was treated for congestive heart failure for the second time. His children travelled from out of town to see him. He knew that this was a chronic disease that would result in his death. He went out in his yard early in the morning when his adult children were asleep.

He called the 911 dispatcher so they would know where to find him and not disturb his children, whom he didn't want to find him, and while still on the phone with her, shot himself after carefully explaining where he was, and why.

Seniors are already dealing with death because of their age. As they become ill, or even just from the process of surviving, they have already lost many of their life companions and friends. The balance of positives to negatives tips the scales towards readiness for death. Waiting alone can seem intolerable. Pain and illness and the costs associated with this can be intolerable. In other countries like Sweden, and in some U.S. states like Oregon, the right of a competent adult to die with dignity and choose assisted end of life options, or even choosing hospice seems a much better option. Many people don't know that hospice services are usually free, and extremely comfortable, much more so than typical nursing home care. Life ending illness are not actively treated, the person is kept very comfortable with as much pain medications as they need, and they have a chance to have a psychologically helpful closing goodbye with family and friends.

My uncle was in his 80s when he took all the sleeping pills he had been saving just before he went to the hospital for his dialysis treatment. He was sick and tired of the treatments and of being ill. His son had told him years before that dying of kidney failure was excruciatingly painful, a white lie intended to get his father to agree to dialysis 10 years earlier. Now he'd had enough, he was tired and weak and ready to die. So he took the overdose before going to the hospital. His intention was to avoid having his family members with whom he lived, from the trauma of finding him dead in their home. When he lapsed into a coma during his treatment, he went right to the ER and was resuscitated. When I explained to him that hospice was a comfortable option and that he would not be in pain, he chose this and ended his life very comfortably, getting to see all those close to him and all getting a chance for a meaningful goodbye. He held court for days eating all the favorite foods he was not allowed for years, surrounded by those who loved him.

High Risk Group: Doctors

While I was still writing this book, a local doctor killed himself. This was a younger psychiatrist with a successful practice, leaving three children after shooting himself in the head. What do you imagine his patients are thinking right now, especially if they are struggling with depression or suicidal thoughts? I didn't know him but thinking about this makes me want to cry.

Did you know that doctors actually have higher rates of suicide than Veterans? Their suicide rate is twice as high as the general population. The number of doctor suicides is estimated to occur at 40 per 100,000. This is more than double what is seen among the American general public, which is thought to be around 13 per 100,000. That works out at between 300 and 400 medical practitioners taking their own lives every single year. In the U.S., health professionals are well compensated and well educated. It is a career choice many wish for but few achieve.

How can you explain suicides among this group? They are smart, educated, and by most standards, successful. They have access to resources. What possible reason could they have for ending their lives? We tend to think of this group as success stories. But there are significant stressors in the training and in these careers.

Doctors endure extended training which is extremely competitive. The training itself is taxing intellectually, emotionally and financially. They usually enter the medical field because they want to help others. While training involves intensive and prolonged exposure to almost intolerable stress, being responsible for another's life is overwhelming.

Because the exposure to stress is so prolonged, talented and compassionate people reach their breaking point. They give up. Doctors tend to feel they should be stronger, and think they're alone in their despair. They don't turn to each other and they don't talk about how they feel, or how afraid they are of failure. They often internalize their despair and end their lives. As humans, doctors are exposed to the same kind of life stressors as others, and deal with it the same way others do, with drugs and alcohol. Their suicide means is usually drug overdose. They have access to drugs and know how much to take.

The loss of physicians yearly to suicide is a tragic loss of resources because we need compassionate people to provide our healthcare. The process of medical training has been inhumane for some time, based on an archaic notion that the quality of the ability to provide treatment is based on one's ability to tolerate extreme stress over long periods of time.

Doctors and nurses are made to suffer,and are stressed to their emotional and physical tolerance as part of training in the belief that this trait is necessary to be successful in the field. Yet that exposure to prolonged sleep deprivation and emotional and physical stress becomes more than some can bear. Students graduate with high student loan amounts.

Adjusting to the work environment coupled with insurance restrictions further frustrates those whose goal it is to help others as it impairs their ability to help those they seek to help. Normal life stressors add to the mix. Relationships suffer with the amount of time lost to studying and working, more so than with a number of other types of employment. Varying work shifts and the need to be "on call" may cause interference with emotional intimacy. The scales can tip to overwhelming. Approximately one million people lose their health provider each year to suicide.

Two physicians have dedicated much of their time and resources to exposing this issue with the hope of improving and reducing these losses. Dr. Pam Wimble is completing a documentary called "Do No Harm" that will likely be released around the time of publication of this book. She personally makes herself available to any medical person experiencing suicidal thoughts. She published the book "Physician Suicide Letters" and personally responds to every email. She offers retreats for professionals to address a number of the burnout issues.

Pam writes "Public perception maintains that doctors are successful, intelligent, wealthy, and immune from the problems of the masses. To patients, it is inconceivable that doctors would have the highest suicide rate of any profession. Even more baffling, "happy" doctors are dying by suicide. Many doctors who kill themselves appear to be the most optimistic, upbeat, and confident people. Just back from Disneyland, just bought tickets for a family cruise, just gave a thumbs up to the team after a successful surgery-and hours later they shoot themselves in the head."

Dr. Kevin Pho also makes himself available personally, and frequently addresses issues related to doctor suicide on his website. These two physicians are making a big difference to those who reach out to them. They both write and do public speaking on the matter. Pam reaches out to doctors and holds mental health retreats designed for their special set of circumstances. She also compiles an ongoing registry, and finds out as much about each case as possible.

Here are some of Dr Wimble's conclusions, written as an article titled "What I've learned from 952 doctor suicides" This article featured in The Washington Post and Chicago Tribune

> *Five years ago today I was at a memorial. Another suicide. Our third doctor in 18 months. Everyone kept whispering, "Why?" I was determined to find out.*
>
> *So I started counting dead doctors. I left the service with a list of 10. Five years later I have 547. [As of 6/17/18] I've got 952 doctor suicides on my registry. If you've lost a doctor or medical student to suicide, please (confidentially*
>
> *Immediately, I began writing and speaking*
>
> *about suicide. So many distressed doctors (and med students) wrote and phoned me. Soon I was running a de facto international suicide hotline from my*

35

home. To date, I've spoken to thousands of suicidal doctors; published a <u>book</u> of their suicide letters (<u>free audiobook</u>); attended more funerals; interviewed surviving physicians, families, and friends. I've spent nearly every waking moment over the past five years on a personal quest for the truth of Why. Here are 35 things I've discovered:

[As of 6/17/18] I've got 952 doctor suicides on my registry. If you've lost a doctor or medical student to suicide, please (confidentially

Immediately, I began writing and speaking about suicide. So many distressed doctors (and med students) wrote and phoned me. Soon I was running a de facto international suicide hotline from my home. To date, I've spoken to thousands of suicidal doctors; published a book of their suicide letters (free audiobook available); attended more funerals; interviewed surviving physicians, families, and friends. I've spent nearly every waking moment over the past five years on a personal quest for the truth of Why.

Here are 35 things I've discovered:

High doctor suicide rates have been

reported since 1858. *Yet more than 150 years later the root causes of these suicides remain unaddressed.*

Physician suicide is a public health crisis. *One million Americans lose their doctors to suicide each year.*

Most doctors have lost a colleague to suicide. *Some have lost up to eight during their career—with no opportunity to grieve.*

We lose way more men than women. *For every woman who dies by suicide in medicine, we lose seven men.(For any men who are suffering, please reach out. You are welcome to attend our retreat.)*

Suicide methods vary by region and gender. *Women prefer to overdose and men choose firearms. Gunshot wounds prevail out west. Jumping is popular in New York City. In India doctors are found hanging from ceiling fans.*

Male anesthesiologists are at highest risk. *Most die by overdose. Many are found dead in hospital call rooms.*

Lots of doctors die in hospitals. *Doctors jump from hospital windows or rooftops. They shoot or stab themselves in hospital parking lots. They're found hanging in hospital chapels. Physicians often choose to die where they've been wounded.*

"Happy" doctors die by suicide. *Many doctors who die by suicide are the happiest most well-adjusted people on the outside. Just back from Disneyland, just bought* *tickets for a family cruise, just gave a thumbs up to the team after a successful surgery—and hours later they shoot themselves in the head. Doctors are masters of disguise. Even fun-loving happy docs who crack jokes and make patients smile all day may be suffering in silence. We are all at risk.*

Doctors' family members are at high risk of suicide. By the same method.
*One physician died using the same gun his son used to kill himself. Kaitlyn Elkins, a star third-year medical student, chose suicide by helium inhalation. One year later her mother Rhonda, died by the same method. At Rhonda's funeral, I asked her husband if he thought his wife and daughter would still be alive had Kaitlyn not pursued medicine. He replied, "Yes. Medical school has killed half my family."***

Suicidal doctors are rarely homicidal.
Of the suicides I've compiled, only 2% (15) involve homicide. Half (7) are male physicians who killed a female spouse/girlfriend (all in health care-4 nurses, a nursing student, pharmacy tech, and dentist). Three male physicians murdered their young children. Another strangled his disabled adult daughter before killing himself. Less than 1% of all

doctor suicides involve homicide of their children. Of the 3 cases involving young children, all suicide victims were having marital/relationship problems with the mother. One also killed the mother.

Doctors have personal problems—like everyone else. *We get divorced, have custody battles, infidelity, disabled children, deaths in our families. Working 100+ hours per week immersed in our patients' pain, we've got no time to deal with our own pain. (Spending so much time at work actually leads to divorce and completely dysfunctional personal lives).*

Patient deaths hurt doctors. A lot. *Even when there's no medical error, doctors may never forgive themselves for losing a patient. Suicide is the ultimate self-punishment.*

Malpractice suits kill doctors. *Humans make mistakes. Yet when doctors make mistakes, they're publicly shamed in court on TV, and in newspapers (that live online forever). We continue to suffer the agony of harming someone else-unintentionally-for the rest of our lives.*

Doctors who do illegal things kill themselves. *Medicare fraud, sex with a patient, DUIs may lead to loss of medical license, prison time, and suicide.*

Academic distress kills medical students' dreams. *Failing boards exams and being unmatched into a specialty of choice has led to suicides.*

Doctors without residencies may die by

39

suicide. *Dr. Robert Chu, unmatched to residency, wrote a letter to medical officials and government leaders calling out the flawed system that undermined his career prior to his suicide.*

Assembly-line medicine kills doctors. *Brilliant, compassionate people can't care for complex patients in 10-minute slots. When punished or fired for "inefficiency" or "low productivity doctors may choose suicide. Pressure from insurance companies and government mandates further crush the souls of these talented people who just want to help their patients. Many doctors cite inhumane working conditions in their suicide notes.*

Sleep deprivation is a (deadly) torture technique. *Physicians have suffered hallucinations, life-threatening seizures, depression, and suicide solely related to sleep deprivation. Sleep-deprived doctors disclose hospital horrors that kill or injure patients. Others die in fatigue- related car crashes after long shifts. Resident physicians are now "capped" at 28-hour shifts and 80-hour weeks. If they "violate" work hours (by caring for patients) they are forced to lie on their time cards or be written up as "inefficient" and sent to a psychiatrist for stimulant medications. Some doctors kill themselves for fear of harming a patient from extreme sleep deprivation.*

Blaming doctors increases suicides.

Words like "burnout" and "resilience" are often employed by medical institutions as psychological warfare to blame and shame doctors while deflecting attention from inhumane working conditions. When doctors are punished for occupationally induced mental health conditions (while underlying human rights violations are not addressed), they become even more hopeless and desperate.

Sweet, sensitive souls are at highest risk. *Some of the most caring, compassionate, and intelligent doctors choose suicide rather than continuing to work in such callous, uncaring and ruthlessly greedy medical corporations.*

Doctors can't get confidential mental health care. *So they drive out of town, pay cash, and use fake names to hide from state medical boards, hospitals, and insurance plans that ask doctors about their mental health care and may then exclude them from state licensure, hospital privileges, and health plan participation. (Even if confidential care were available, physicians have little time to access care when working 80 100+ hours per week).*

Doctors have trouble caring for doctors. *Doctors treat physician patients differently by downplaying psychiatric issues to protect physicians from medical board mental health investigations. Untreated mental health conditions may lead to suicide.*

Medical board investigations increase suicide risk. *One doctor hanged himself from a tree outside the Florida medical board office after being denied his license. He was told to "come back in a year and we will reinstate your license." Meanwhile he lost everything and was living in a halfway house.*

Physician Health Programs (PHPs) may increase suicide risk. *Forcing doctors with occupationally induced mental health issues into these 12-step programs with witnessed random urine drug screens (when they've never had a drug problem!) is humiliating and unethical. So doctors hide their mental health conditions for fear of being punished by PHPs. [Note: PHPs have helped some doctors with substance abuse especially]*

Substance abuse is a late-stage effect of lack of mental health care. *Since doctors may lose their license for seeking mental health care or get locked into PHPs; they self-medicate with alcohol, illicit drugs, or self- prescribe psychotropic medications.*

Doctors develop on-the-job PTSD.
Especially true in emergency medicine. Then one day they "snap".

Cultural taboos reinforce secrecy.
Suicide is a sin in many religions. Islam and Christian families have asked that I

42

hide the suicides of family members.
Indian families often claim a suicide is a
homicide or an accident, even when it's
obviously self-inflicted.

Media offers incomplete coverage of
suspicious deaths. *Articles about doctors*
found dead in hospital call rooms claim
"no foul play." No follow-up stories.

Medical schools and hospitals lie (or
omit the truth) to cover up suicides-even
when media and family report cause of
death. *Medical student Ari Frosch stood*
in front of a train, yet his school reported
he died at home with his family. Though
the family of psychiatrist Christine Petrich
shared that she bought a gun and killed
herself (after just getting her hair done and
planning a surprise trip to Lego Land and
Disney for her kids) on their GoFundMe
page, her employer wrote she "passed
away." Shouldn't the department of
psychiatry take a more active interest in
physician suicide?

Euphemisms cover up doctor suicides.
Suicide is omitted from obituaries,
funerals, clinics, hospitals, and medical
schools. Instead we hear "passed away
unexpectedly in her sleep" and "he went to
be with the Lord."

Secrets will not save us. *We're unlikely to*
make a medical breakthrough on a hidden
medical condition.

Doctors choose suicide to end their pain (not because they want to die). *Suicide is preventable. We can help doctors who are suffering if we stop with all the secrecy and punishment.*

I've been shunned for speaking about doctor suicide. *After being invited by the AMA to deliver my TEDMED talk, I was disinvited shortly before the event because they were "uncomfortable" with physician suicide."*

** Author's Note: Rhonda Sellers Elkins lost her daughter to suicide while in medical school.

Rhonda was a nurse, and wrote a book about losing her daughter called "My Bright Shining Star; A Mother's True Story of Brilliance, Love and Suicide." Rhonda Sellers Elkins worked hard to recover by writing this book and working as a suicide prevention advocate, but did not survive this horrible loss of her daughter, and took her own life in 2014, using the same means as her daughter.)

An honest obituary from Dr Wimble's blog:

"Christopher Chad Dawson NORTH RICHLAND HILLS--On the morning of Saturday, Dec. 9, 2017, Christopher Chad Dawson lost the battle of severe depression. After years of suffering with anxiety, depression set hold and Chris was unable to escape its clutch.
MEMORIAL SERVICE: 2 p.m. Thursday, Northgate Church. He found happiness in teaching Luke sport skills and watching him at his sport games. He helped Luke through a lot of his anxiety, but was overwhelmed with the thought of Luke growing up to be like him. Bree was his littleprincess and he never wanted to go to bed without a kiss and big hug. His children adored him and he adored them. Chris worked hard to overcome his anxiety. He obtained his business degree frpm TCU before deciding he wanted to commit his life to medicine. He sacrificed fun, free time, and relaxation to receive his medical degree in UTHSCSA. He then took on the challenge of surgical residency in Phoenix, Ariz. Between his ever-present anxiety, long work hours and intense stress, the Chris we knew and loved began to fade. Chris and Rachel started having extreme marital problems, but the children were always loved above all. He managed to make it through residency, but was damaged and attempted to self-medicate

his hurt. He fought to get out of the deep, deep hole he was in but was afraid of the repercussion of his career if he were to get professional help. He felt hopeless, worthless, and trapped. On Saturday morning, while not in his right mind, he did the unimaginable. But that was not the Chris his family and friends knew and loved. Chris was an intelligent surgeon, a loving father who had so much to offer the world. But the sick disease of depression, anxiety and addiction did not allow him to continue the journey. SURVIVORS: Survived by his wife, Rachel Williams Dawson; parents, Ken and Joyce Dawson of Burleson; brothers, Jeremy and wife, Bianca Dawson, Colton Dawson and Michael and wife, Becky Timberlake; and a multitude of extended family."

Here's what stopped this doctor's suicidal thoughts, by Thomas L. Watson, MD August 30, 2018.

"Once your kids are older, please encourage them to get help if they start with your symptoms," Dr. K soberly instructed me recently. This came after a roller-coaster ride over the past year to sort out and treat my increasing and overwhelming desire to shoot myself in the head.

Although the cause of suicidality varies from person to person, this is my story.

I'm a happily married 59-year-old general practitioner. Both of our adult children have completed college and are gainfully employed. There was no one I wanted to hurt with my death.

For the longest time, I thought I had allergic conjunctivitis. As it turned out, once the crying and fighting the urge to cry resolved with Effexor, my conjunctiva cleared-up. Frankly, I have always questioned the validity of fibromyalgia, until I started with symptoms. Then, just like my "allergic conjunctivitis," Effexor also gave me relief of my chronic upper back and neck trigger points, fatigue, sleep, memory, and mood issues ... so much for my own diagnostic skills. Unfortunately, there was no real change in my suicidality with Effexor. Only the frequency lessened to a few times a day.

I knew I was depressed, really depressed. I was ignoring and fighting these feelings ever since I was a young adult because there was no reason for my sadness. I was embarrassed because my childhood was so great. I felt I never suffered enough to become depressed; I felt like a spoiled brat, crying for no reason.

During my neurosurgical rotation as a surgical resident, I felt differently when the ER paged me regarding a patient with a self-inflicted gunshot wound to the head. I lacked the profound sadness that I had for other patients that died by any other means. There was a morbid sense of solace and closure for these predominantly twenty- something males. Neither the family chaos in the waiting room nor lack of an organ donor card really touched my heart. In retrospect, I was callous and selfish. My maternal great-grandfather took his life with his shotgun loaded with a slug. But not before telling his son (my grandfather) his plans. He was an octogenarian, and the DMV sent him a notice that he could no longer drive. My grandfather did nothing to prevent it. In fact, he shared the story with me as a young teenager. He told me that he planned the same, "when the time came."

Zeus is a three-year-old Belgian Malinois,

trained to be a service dog for Leysh, one of the medical assistants at our clinic. He has been with us since he was a puppy. A couple of years ago, I was contemplating shooting myself. I had a Sig Sauer P238 at work. It was a bad day, a terrible day. We have always joked that Zeus has ADHD – it's a Mal thing. So, when he came into my office and placed his head on my lap, looking up at me with a concerned expression which I have never seen before, I still thought he just wanted to play, but he didn't move for over 15 minutes. Only when my bad thought started to subside as I was petting his head, Zeus left, only to return with his favorite bone and placed it in my lap. Then he brought and put his favorite toy at my feet. He finally laid down at my feet, keeping me company. Watching over me.

It was a few weeks later when Leysh got into trouble with me regarding a non-work-related issue. She is like a daughter to my wife and me. We argued, then I asked her to promise never again to do what she did. She said, "I can't promise that, but will promise to try ... if you promise me something." I asked her what it was. "Get rid of Megan's handgun and never get another one." She broke down in tears and said, "Because I don't want you to shoot yourself." In tears, I assured her I was only sad and would never shoot myself – I agreed to her terms.

*How Zeus and Leysh knew, I'll never know,
but I needed to get help.*

*That phone call was the first time I ever
told anyone about my suicidality. I was so
embarrassed and felt "broken." Dr. K's
receptionist told me that his next
appointment for a new patient was 6
months out. I asked if I could leave him a
message, and she said, "Yes." On the
message, I mentioned that I'm a 58-year
old physician with strong suicidal ideation.
The receptionist called back the next day
and made me an appointment for 3 weeks,
which was still quite a stretch. For being a
simple task, it was the hardest call I have
made in years. At the same time, I felt
hope. It was the longest 3 weeks.*

*Dr. K is a portly 78-year-old wizard of
psychiatry. His clinic is an old, dimly lit
converted home furnished with tattered
swap-meet-caliber furniture. Maybe even
a borderline hoarder. Every waiting room
chair was filled with disheveled patients
with flat affects and overt psychiatric
pathology. Patients were also standing
outside smoking partially smoked
cigarettes they found nearby. I felt out of
place and comfortable at the same time.*

*His endearing compassionate concern was
remarkable. He had tears welling up as I
shared my medical history. Dr. K assured
me that my suicidality was secondary to
severe major depressive disorder and*

50

started me on Effexor.

The following week I told him with enthusiasm that my red, irritated eye and other psychosomatic symptoms resolved. I also shared that my wife and I have been together since high school. Together we have tackled a lot of stressful events; almost losing our newborn son with hereditary nephrogenic diabetes insipidus and losing our home in the California cedar fire to name just a few. So, Jaleh knew what to do. She removed all firearms from the house and did everything she could to decrease any external stressors that came our way.

Over the next few months, I slowly increased my dosage of Effexor. Unfortunately, the side effects made it hard to be compliant, so Dr. K switched me to Wellbutrin which had no adverse issues, but I had a relapse of my depression and suicidality. It came back with a vengeance.

Up to that time, I was running from the urge to end my life, then with this relapse, I couldn't run any longer, so I started to prepare and plan my death. Dr. K restarted the Effexor and kept me on Wellbutrin. Additionally, he wanted to hospitalize me for 2 weeks. Having a private practice, I couldn't be away for that long. What would be different in treatment besides preventing me from

*killing myself? Dr. K said, "That's exactly
what I want to prevent." We finally agreed
on a promise not to kill myself, but if I
needed to break the promise, I would call
him. I also agreed to a 3-day stay in the
hospital for ECT treatment in the near
future.*

*The following week, Dr. K wanted to first
start Lithium before ECT. I always
thought Lithium was only for bipolar
treatment; I was wrong. Five days later, it
was like someone turned the switch off in
my brain for suicidality. A switch which
has been on for my entire adult life. Just
as I wouldn't jump into a pit of
rattlesnakes, I now would never put the
muzzle of a loaded pistol against my
temporal bone and pull the trigger.*

*A couple of weeks later, Dr. K asked me
what kept me from taking my own life. I
told him it was my four girls and a dog; my
wife, my daughter, Leysh (like a daughter),
French (like family) who also works with
me, and Zeus who had canine instincts to
keep me safe.*

*There is no doubt, Dr. K saved my life.
With his advanced age, I needed to know
when he planned to retire. He said he
already has plans once he cures all his
patients. But on a serious note, the wait
time to see a psychiatrist is unacceptable.
We need to groom a lot more Dr. Ks
because I suspect my story is the tip of a*

curable iceberg that is melting too fast.

*Yes, I'm still embarrassed about my
diagnosis and the fact I remain on Effexor,
Wellbutrin, and Lithium. To date, only a
handful of people know this dark side of
me. Having equivocal thoughts about
writing this article, I thought about the fact
that the rate of physician suicides is
highest of any profession and exceeds that
of our military, yet we don't hear much
about this "epidemic" in the United States.
And I don't want to be embarrassed
anymore – maybe this will help. Perhaps it
helps to remove the stigma when the time
comes to discuss the genetic component of
suicidality with my kids. Either way, a
long life of embarrassment will suit my
family and me well.*

Thomas L. Watson, MD, is a physician who lives and
practices in San Diego. Watson attended Centro De
Estudios Universitarios Xochicalco in Mexico and is
certified by the American Board of Urgent Care
Medicine. Published in Medpage Today 8/30/18.

Dr. Kevin Pho is a leading speaker, and blogger on
many issues including doctor's committing suicide.
His blog and twitter feed frequently report and address
these issues, and invite others to share there as well.
He is also a physician who is personally trying to
address the issue.

Robyn Symon's documentary on physician suicide

called "Do No Harm" is expected to be released in 2018. Many physicians and this documentary will help call attention to this issue and hopefully address some of the preventable reasons why these occur. Our society needs to do something to prevent those highly trained to help others because we already suffer a great shortage of good providers nationwide.

Author's note:: On a personal note, I break all the "rules" of treatment by honestly telling my suicidal patients how their suicides would affect me. I think this has reduced the number of those who have ended their lives under my care. They are always surprised to hear that it would affect me at all. I explain to them that every time I've lost a patient, I've considered stopping what I do for a living, and that it affects me deeply. I see each loss as a personal failure, but I also understand and accept I can't help everyone choose life. I want to be clear that according to most educational resources on the subject, what I'm doing by sharing my own personal feelings with a patient is considered "taboo" in the medical profession. However, I've lost a particularly low number of patients to suicide compared to those of my colleagues. I've truly lost only one patient to suicide and three to accidental overdoses. These are profiled in the Chapter 6 Case Studies. I think sharing how their decision would affect me has given suicidal patients pause in carrying their plans forward. So I will continue to do this. I believe sharing how it would affect you when you're dealing with someone who is depressed and suicidal is one of the strongest tools we have in prevention of suicide deaths. When people seriously or flippantly make comments about suicide, I never miss an opportunity to address this in a personal and intimate way. Helping the person who is suicidal think about the impact on others, helps reconnect them with the world from which they feel estranged. As we will talk about more in the prevention chapter 3, connectedness to others is vitally important to quality of life.

High Risk Group: Substance use, Addiction, Chronic pain, Pain meds

It turns out that science is now showing that there is a genetic inherited predisposition to addiction that in the future will be tested so the people who carry this trait will be more aware of the risks of substance addiction. That knowledge will help prevent some but not all addiction. Pain medication dependence and abuse is an epidemic in the United States. The Drug Enforcement Agency has been cracking down and pulling licenses of physicians who continue to prescribe large amounts of opiate drugs chronically (further adding to the crisis, and the difficulties of being a physician). The agency is requiring prescribers to have plans to reduce use over time and limit quantities, and have specific training in pain management that patients have to be engaged in, so that other forms of pain management are used rather than prescribing opiates chronically. But that crackdown without viable alternatives is likely to create more problems. Those who are addicted are likely to find other more lethal forms of drugs to control their addictions, like heroin, until some real alternatives are found to this problem.

Going off opiates is incredibly difficult. Many types of pain are chronic, and chronic pain is a risk factor in developing depression and anxiety. Those in pain not relieved by the available drugs are more likely to try to potentiate their medication by adding alcohol, greatly increasing the risks of accidental overdose deaths. The process of reducing use and dependence on these medications is extremely difficult, expensive, and painful. Many people who get exposed to these medications for short term use that is appropriate such as after an accident or a surgery, have no idea how quickly they will become dependent or how difficult it will be to stop using. The cravings, the quieting of the brain, the peace of relief from pain, all these factors will make it difficult to stop use. The medications that might be involved in treatment of these addictions might be too cost prohibitive or time consuming. Methadone and Suboxone are frequently prescribed, but require frequent visits (initially daily for Methadone) and often aren't covered by Health Insurance. It is less expensive to buy heroin rather than go daily to a Methadone clinic. It makes a great deal of sense to focus on preventing misuse in the early part of treatment, but if you're a person suffering from chronic pain, your choices for relief are very limited. You are literally between a rock and a hard place.

Although addiction is a physical and chemical issue, there is a lot of failure in trying to avoid the addictive substance. Anyone who works with addiction patients knows there is a lot of relapse, and with failure comes shame. While addiction specialists understand that this is a long and difficult process, the people around the sufferer aren't as likely to be as accepting. Employers find the interruption in work productivity too disruptive to work flow and jobs are lost. Spouses resent the emotional and financial toll, the chronic disappointments, and the costs. It can lead to a series of failures that can end relationships and lives. It takes a lot of strength and courage to endure the recovery process and succeed. The physical and emotional process of recovery can just seem too hard or overwhelming, and people give up. The substance itself reduces the inhibition and the shame contributes to a feeling of "I may as well end my life."
Even without addiction, substance use of any kind

reduces inhibitions. Thus, any kind of substance use in an already depressed or distraught person can reduce their inhibition to act on their thoughts. Well-meaning friends and family can encourage one to "go out and have fun and forget about a recent loss", or "have a drink, you'll feel better", when this is exactly the most dangerous thing you can say to anyone going through a depressive period or a serious loss.

Many people with substance problems have gotten into substance abuse because they felt so much pain they were trying to numb themselves from. That doesn't make you a bad person if that has happened to you. No one who hasn't been through this understands how difficult of a process it is to get sober. It's usually not easy and it usually takes many attempts to be successful. Failing at something over and over again doesn't make your life or you unworthy or unlovable. You are loveable. Many people love you who want you to succeed at this, even if they have turned their backs on you because of past failures, they are just waiting to bring you into the fold of life again. Don't give up.Keep trying. Every day is a new day to try. All of them will welcome you back or others will who will take their place. Others who have recovered understand the pain you have gone through and the incredible effort it takes to survive that. Surround yourself and seek out those who understand.

If you love someone who is currently trying to get sober, it's an exhausting and long process. It's hard to know how long to hope and hold on and when to let go. Get involved with Alanon to help you sort out this process and get yourself support. It isn't the person you hate, it's the disease. It takes a lot of strength and support for you to keep this clear. You will also need help to get through this. If you need to let go of the relationship, you have to have help to forgive yourself and forgive the person who has put you through this trial. Any way you look at this, it's not a black and white situation. People want clear black/white solutions to things and this isn't possible. Those close to you are likely not to understand. You will need to get help so you can survive this process. People are not disposable. No one chooses to be in the painful throes of an addiction, and despite their desire to change, it is extremely difficult. You can't do it alone.

Autocide and Other "accidents"

Autocide is the term used for a suspicious death, especially when it is a single car accident and a death results. Most autocides are never publicized as being suicides. My son told me about someone he knew, who had just relapsed on drugs shortly after getting out of rehab. He was discovered, got in an argument and took off in the car speeding on a wet road in excess of 100 miles per hour. He died by his car hydroplaning into a tree shortly afterwards. His was an autocide but the coroners ruling was accidental death. The family still whispers about it today, and no one talks openly about this as being a suicide. Many of us know of such situations. The family escapes the stigma of suicide, but the secret is another burden along with the loss.

There have also been some studies to suggest that when substances are involved in fatal car crashes, there are often thoughts of suicide in the drivers who caused the accidents. Their intention was not to kill someone else, but to kill themselves. I see a professional truck driver today who is still traumatized by the young woman who took her life by driving straight on into his truck. It would be very interesting if we were able to evaluate real statistics about how often this really occurs.

High Risk Group: Bullying

In recent years, a series of bullying-related suicides in the U.S. and across the globe have drawn attention to the connection between bullying and suicide. Though too, many adults still see bullying as "just part of being a kid. Yet, it is a serious problem that leads to many negative effects for victims, including suicide. Many people may not realize that there is also a link between being the bully and committing suicide.

Teens with any other sexual orientation other than heterosexual have much higher rates of suicide attempts and completed suicide among this young group. The rates of suicide among homosexual, bisexual, and transgender youth are 3.5 times those of the rest of the teens, with transgender youth having the highest rates. The suicides are caused by bullying.

Statistics of bullying and suicide

- Suicide is the third leading cause of death among young people, resulting in about 4,400 deaths per year, according to the CDC. For every suicide among young people, there are at least 100 suicide attempts. Over 14 percent of high school students have considered suicide, and almost 7 percent have attempted it.

- Bully victims are between 2 to 9 times more likely to consider suicide than non-victims, according to studies by Yale University

- A study in Britain found that at least half of suicides among young people are related to bullying.

- 10 to 14 year old girls may be at even higher risk for suicide, according to the study above.

- According to statistics reported by ABC News, nearly 30 percent of students are either bullies or victims of bullying, and 160,000 kids stay home from school every day because of fear of bullying.".

- Nearly 9 out of 10 LGBTQ youth report being verbally harassed at school in the past year because of their sexual orientation.

- 57% of boys and 43% of girls reported being bullied because of religious or cultural differences.

- Bullies often go on to perpetrate violence later in life: 40% of boys identified as bullies in grades 6 through 9 had three or more arrests by age 30.

- One out of every 10 students who drop out of school does so because of repeated incidents of bullying.

- 75% of shooting incidents at schools have been linked to bullying and harassment.

- 64% of children who were bullied did not report it.

- Nearly 70% of students think schools respond poorly to   bullying.

- When bystanders intervene, bullying stops within 10 seconds 57% of the time.

Bully-related suicide can be connected to any type of bullying, including physical bullying, emotional bullying, cyberbullying, and sexting, or circulating suggestive or nude photos or messages about a person. We currently are at an even more alarming level of bullying in our country, when our 45th President does this as a matter of daily record, and people in power stand by and make no effort to correct it. The inherent message becomes that this is acceptable behavior, and victims feel isolated and hopeless.

High Risk Group: Celebrity suicides; Traumatic Brain Injury, and the Copy Cat Effect

Consider that I started writing this book in 2014. When I began, Robin Williams was still alive. Kate Spade and Anthony Bourdain hadn't yet hung themselves. There is a lot of attention when celebrities kill themselves, and there is always concern about the copycat effect. This effect occurs at some time at almost every high school in America. One person's suicide can often trigger someone else's.

Robin Williams' suicide touched more people than any other public suicide previous or since. It was one of the calls to action that brought me back to completing this book. I credit his suicide with bringing this social issue to the public's attention, and inviting much more public discussion about suicide than had ever occurred before. He was beloved, and he made us laugh for so many years. What could have possibly triggered such a choice?

Many actors suicide due to the immense pressure of that field and the rarity of sustained success. But Robin was not that kind of actor. He was able to maintain professional success over 40 years, and was still very loved, both in the media and in his personal life.

Because he was a comedian, it's easy to think, gee, he was so successful and so funny, if he couldn't find a reason to live, how can I?

Robin Williams' situation might have been very different than the other actor suicides; one article said that he had been given a diagnosis of Lewy Body Dementia. Lewy Body is a rare and particularly awful type of dementia, and I hope you never have the experience of watching this up front and personal. A woman I was treating suddenly developed particularly severe psychotic issues at night. She exhibited all the symptoms of schizophrenia, however this is not a disease that suddenly manifests itself in later life, nor is it one that severely worsens at a particular time of the day. It turned out to be Lewy Body dementia. As predicted, this woman died within a year of her diagnosis. Within 6 months, she was essentially catatonic and wheelchair bound. Prior to this, she had terrifying hallucinations that would keep her and her family up all night, with her constantly calling the police for help. She had to be strongly sedated to control her behavior. If Robin Williams looked up the diagnosis, prognosis, and course of this disease, it wouldn't be surprising for him to want to spare himself and his loved ones this ordeal. Presence of terminal illness is a common factor involved in the decision to suicide.

This is very different from the situation with Kate Spade. Her sister later reported that Kate had alcohol issues and very likely had been living with Bipolar disorder for many years. The final straw was likely her husband asking for a divorce. Here the risk factors were untreated mental illness, substance abuse, and a life crisis. Again, completely different is the situation with Anthony Bourdain. As of the writing of this passage, no particular life crises were identified. Anthony had a history of substance issues but this was well controlled. He was on some medication for some mental illness suggesting he was in treatment. No impending stress or crisis was the trigger. But perhaps the death of Kate Spade was influential, since he chose the same method of death that she had. Here, perhaps it was the copycat effect in a person who though successful, also struggled with his emotions for many years.

Unless you live in Chicago, or are a big football fan, you might not know of Dave Duerson. He was a safety on the Chicago Bears in the National Football League.

He played on their Super Bowl winning team in 1985 and he was featured in the movie "Concussion." After Duerson retired from playing football, he became a successful businessman. He also became a player representative on the panel that considered retired players' claims under the NFL.'s disability plan and the "88 Plan", a fund that helps retired players with dementia. According to the book and movie based on the studies of neuropathologist Bennet Omalu, a pathologist who researched chronic traumatic encephalopathy, it was believed at that time that football didn't cause any brain injury. The NFL hired physicians who agreed with them to sit on their panels. Although Dave's family says the movie misrepresented his father, Duerson Duerson testified at 2007 congressional hearings that focused on whether the NFL disability board was unfairly denying benefits. He testified that there was no proven link between playing football and developing dementia, he fought against the player claims. Dr. Bennet Omalu, the neuropathologist who identified and fought for the recognition of the presence and effects of chronic traumatic encephalopathy, was the doctor who the NFL tried to discredit. He turned out to be correct and much research is going on now that chronic non-concussive brain injury can cause serious consequences over time. One of those serious effects appears to be severe mental health issues which has resulted in numerous suicides in athletes who likely were suffering.

Here are just a few of the NFL players affected by Chronic Traumatic Encephalopathy or "CTE."

- A postmortem analysis of the brain of Jovan Belcher, the Chiefs linebacker who killed his girlfriend in December 2012 in a murder-suicide, found that the 25- year-old linebacker probably was suffering from CTE. He is among the youngest known players to have the disease.

- New York Giants safety Tyler Sash, 27, died of an accidental overdose of medications in September. His mother, who had seen his irregular behavior and periods of confusion and memory loss, said her son knew something was wrong. It was CTE, which had advanced to a stage rarely seen in someone his age.

▪ Former New York Giants running back and broadcaster Frank Gifford, who died in 2015, had CTE, as his family had suspected.

▪ Ray Easterling, a former safety for the Atlanta Falcons, was depressed and suffering from apparent dementia when he shot himself in 2012 at age 62. An autopsy found CTE in his brain. "It amazed me to think about what he dealt with every day inside his head," said his widow, Mary Ann.

▪ San Diego Chargers linebacker Junior Seau, who suffered from CTE, shot himself in 2012 at the age of 43.

Dr. Omalu has estimated that more than 90 percent of all NFL players have CTE. The disease, however, can only be diagnosed after death. Omalu suspects OJ Simpson is probably suffering from the disease, saying Simpson's "irrationality, his impulsivity ... his sexual improprieties, his violent tendencies, domestic violence history" as signs of the disease."

These headlines point out to us that the prevalence of brain injury in athletes is likely a much more serious health risk than we realize at this time. The disease can lead to behaviors, such as a previously kind person becoming aggressive, irrational, and violent leading to a loss in their personal support system, than we have previously recognized. A previously happy go lucky person can become severely and intractably depressed with no relief. The brain is a fragile organ and can be easily injured, and the results of injuries might not be apparent for decades.

Suicides often occur in clusters. The impact of one suicide can lead to similar behaviors in others, and is a phenomenon that is not new, but is of more concern because of how far and fast information travels today. A vulnerable person hears of another suicide, and emulates it. This phenomenon is one of the reasons people don't like to publicize suicides, but the whispers continue whether it is or isn't discussed. Because the incidence of one suicide can lead to similar behavior by others, it is important to talk openly about suicide when it occurs, especially if you fear someone nearby is struggling with similar emotional issues. Suicide clusters are more likely to occur in those under the age of 25, but happen in a variety of groups. Students, prison populations, minority groups who feel discriminated and marginalized by society, soldiers, teens, even celebrities are not immune to this response. Intervention has been shown to be effective, when a supportive community comes together to provide resources and support to those likely to be traumatized by a recent suicide.

Sources:

Suicide Among Veterans and Other Americans 2001-
2014, Office of Suicide Prevention. Updated August
2017 by the Office of Mental Health and Suicide
Prevention, US Department of Veterans Affairs
(referred to multiple times in chapter 2)

Curtin SC, Warner M., Geedegaard H. Increase in
Suicide in the United States 1999-2014. NCHS data
brief, no 241. National Center for Health Statistics
2016

"Adolescent Suicide Myths in the United States"
Moskos, Achilles, and Gray. From Crisis 2004,
Volume 25 (4):176-182

"We Need to Talk About Kids and Smartphones".
Time Magazine, Nov.6, 2017. By Markham Heid.

"The number of teens who are depressed is soaring-
and all signs point to smartphones" by Jean Twenge.
Nov. 18, 2017. Business Insider.

"Reducing Risk When Prescribing For Children and
Adolescents" Published by PRMS, based on a seminar
presentation given by Kim Masters MD, 10/2015

Dr. Kevin Pho M.D. from KevinMD.com excerpts
reprinted with permission. co-author of the book,
Establishing, Managing, and Protecting Your Online
Reputation: A Social Media Guide for Physicians and
Medical Practices

Dr Pamela Wible pioneered the community-designed
ideal medical clinic and blogs at Ideal Medical Care.
She is the author of Physician Suicide Letters —

Answered . Excerpts reprinted with permission.

Robyn Symon is the filmmaker of the upcoming documentary "Do No Harm". She is a two-time Emmy Award-winner, and an accomplished writer, producer/director, and editor.

www.bullyingstatistics.org/ American Journal of Psychiatry

Luby J, et al "A randomized controlled trial of parent-child psychotherapy targeting emotion development for early childhood depression" Am J Psychiatry 2018; DOI: 10.1176/appi.ajp.2018.18030321.

JAMA Pediatrics

Source Reference: Di Giacomo E, et al "Estimating the risk of attempted suicide among sexual minority youths" JAMA Pediatr 2018; DOI: 10.1001/jamapediatrics.2018.2731.

Luby J, et al "A randomized controlled trial of parent-child psychotherapy targeting emotion development for early childhood depression" Am J Psychiatry 2018; DOI: 10.1176/appi.ajp.2018.18030321.

JAMA Pediatrics

Source Reference: Di Giacomo E, et al "Estimating the risk of attempted suicide among sexual minority youths" JAMA Pediatr 2018; DOI:

Chapter 2: Suicide Misinformation and Myths

"It's not normal to think about suicide"

In our lifetimes, 20 % of humans will experience a major depressive episode and feel miserable enough to think of ending their life. That's one in five of us. No, thinking about death and suicide is not abnormal. It is on the news all the time, famous people are doing it. Kids in schools are dying this way. Suicide crosses almost everyone's mind, and it not abnormal to think about it, especially when you're struggling.

In my office when I ask this, almost everyone denies thinking about it, but I know at least half of them do. Genetic science has tentatively identified a genetic marker that may predict which half we are. Suicide rates have also been linked nationally with the amount of trace lithium in drinking water. Communities with higher Lithium levels have lower suicide rates. Why don't we add Lithium to all multivitamins? Because Lithium has a connection to bipolar treatment, and a bad record of toxicity when high doses were used clinically in the past. Both the genetic and Lithium factors support neurobiological factors are connected to suicide.

Of course, many psychosocial factors are also involved in thinking about suicide. Knowing our lives are finite is probably one of the most difficult things about being human. We are the only known species who lives their lives aware of their mortality. It's a dilemma, we both, at times don't want to live with the pain while also don't want to die. The more freedoms we have in our life, the easier and more complicated our lives become. Free time can provide more time to think about things that are difficult. Our emotions can be overwhelming. Comparing ourselves to others makes us feel like a failure. Social media posts and media in general promote successes, very few people share their vulnerabilities or failures. It's hard to read what's published or reported on TV and social media and not compare ourselves to an airbrushed ideal that is shared with the public. Our society is more mobile and fragmented than it has ever been before. With more and more single parent homes and two working parent homes, emotional development can be overlooked when drained and exhausted parents come home. We repeat the maladaptive patterns of our parents, and maladaptive functioning then repeats from generation to generation. American society depends on parents to teach life skills, but when parents are stressed and struggling themselves, where is this new information and training for them?

It is not abnormal to think about our mortality, and it is not abnormal to fantasize about escaping our troubles when they're overwhelming. Somehow we have to work as a society to take this topic out of secrecy and make it okay to talk about feeling fragile.

Traditional psychiatry focused on pathology, but modern psychology has been studying the factors involved in happiness and mental health. There has been tremendous growth in this area for years, but there has been a tremendous lag about getting this information out to the public. This information fostering mental health is life changing. How different all our lives would be if we were all instructed on these skills in school along with mathematics in schools. Until that happens, we need to find out all the ways we can impact and foster our own and others' positive mental health, and we need to learn to do this soon before more precious lives are lost.

Anyone who knows a fellow human is struggling should try to reach out to them and invite them to talk about what they're thinking, and to try to do this without judgment. When we hear young people taking their lives we have to be careful what we say, and try to avoid judgmental comments that would scare our children from talking honestly to us. Contradictory to what's commonly thought, asking someone if they are thinking of taking their life does not put that idea in someone's head. Talking about suicides can encourage people to talk about what they're thinking. I think many parents and teachers and family get too afraid to ask, because they don't know what they will do if the answer is yes. I will answer that question in a number of sections in this book, specifically in Chapter 3. But we really do need as a society to learn to ask this question of each other when we see each other struggling through hard times.

When I was first starting out working in psychiatry, one of my first volunteer jobs was manning a suicide hotline. It was an interesting and sometimes frightening job. But talking someone through this, getting them to agree to speak with someone close to them, and connecting them with someone who could help them was gratifying. These hotlines still do exist today, and exist in phone, text and email formats. The increased attention on celebrity suicides, and veteran suicides has helped these sites to be publicized again. Suicidal thoughts need to be a subject all people feel comfortable talking about. We have to get better at allowing each other to feel okay about imperfect thoughts and feelings. We need to put the technology down, to take the time to listen to each other, and be with each other. True connectedness to others, the knowledge that we are there for them no matter what they've done or thought or how different they think they are, those are the ways we can, as a society, save lives.

Because some people are born to difficult life situations, or have different biochemistry than others, it's not unusual to go through life depressed and not even be aware of it. Recently a patient was referred to me because she took a screening tool for a medical procedure, and it indicated a very high level of depression. Although nothing about this woman's appearance or functioning suggested depression, when quantified using a validated professional testing tool, the level of depression was truly and extremely high!

How does that happen? First, we get conditioned to telling everyone we're "fine", which is just a meaningless pleasantry we exchange. Second, many of us believe feeling depressed indicates a flaw in our personality or emotions, so we don't tell anyone how we truly feel. There are a lot of people walking around who feel that mood is a matter of weak character rather than a brain disease. Major depressive disorder is a debilitating brain disease which vast implications for life, health, and functioning. Major depressive disorder is visible because it involves an acute change from how we usually feel and behave. There are those who deal with daily and long standing chronic depression because of neurotransmitter issues that are inherited, and these people won't exhibit those changes in appetite, functioning, or appearance, and may not even be aware that they are depressed, because it's how they've always felt!

If you're one of those people, depression is a long standing struggle that can get better or worse with stress in your life. It requires us to take extremely good care of our physical and mental health. It requires us to self- monitor because we can slip easily from struggle into darker and more dangerous thoughts. If this describes you, you need medication to correct your neurotransmitter imbalance so that most of the time you are experiencing some pleasure and quality to your life. There is danger to your health in not treating this as the medical condition it is. One is that, in response to external stressors, the balance to endure and live with that internal struggle can dip too low. In a full depressive period or in response to increased stress, the feat to keep functioning can feel insurmountable. I have come to the conclusion that depression is not unlike other mental illnesses in that it causes you to think and feel things that are not based in reality; you can feel things are too painful to endure, and that it won't end. That's truly a mistake in your logic, because the events external to us do always change.

Mental illnesses like depression can be confusing. While you would never argue with your doctor about treating your diabetes and taking medication, we often fight the idea to take medication to treat this disorder. But without treatment, your functioning is harder, your relationships are harder, and your health will suffer from the quiet internal stress you bear; eventually this will lead to other physical illness (gastric illness is most common). Often people are already experiencing these illnesses when they seek treatment for depression. Your medical doctor has to know about all health conditions. They can provide an antidepressant, but a specialist in the field of psychiatry will be able to explain to you why the medication works a certain way and be better informed to provide the right medication at the right dose to help your specific issues. Your brain is important to your overall health and functioning. It matters! A drug won't fix everything wrong in your life. You still have to do additional work to keep your brain and life healthy. But don't add the burden of trying to forego medications if you've already been dealing with depression for a long time. Life is challenging enough already, take good care of yourself and get what you need for your health.

"Won't asking someone if they're thinking about suicide put that idea in their head?"

Sometimes we're aware of people around us going through a tremendously difficult time and we know they're depressed. This could even be a close family member. Do we ever ask them if they're thinking of suicide? That seems like a very difficult question to ask. If they say no, are they just lying to us? What would we do if they said yes? The question itself becomes too frightening to even ask, so we're afraid to. If someone asked you this question today, do you think it would cause you to think about suicide? Not unless it was already on your mind.

We need to begin asking the question a lot more. The truth is that if the person is not thinking of suicide, and look at you like you're crazy to ask that, you can relax. Their response will reduce your worries. They're one of the population that would never consider this. Lucky you. Either their religious beliefs would never allow this, or they're genetically not programmed that way. Whew, you can move on to addressing how to help them otherwise.

If they are thinking of suicide, you know that you need to make sure they're going to therapy or seeing someone who can help them find the right medications, as well as making yourself available seeing them more often, have a safety plan, and perhaps even have them stay with you for a while. People who are engaged in treatment, and have a decent social support network have much lower suicide rates than those suffering from depression not in treatment, without support.

"But what about all those warnings about taking those medications? They can cause people to have suicidal thoughts who didn't have them before? How can medication be a good idea if one of the risks of antidepressants is that it can worsen suicidal thoughts? What is the point of taking a medicine that can make me feel worse?"

People are often afraid of antidepressants because of two issues: fear of feeling like a "zombie" or fear that they won't help and could make them feel worse. I can address both of those concerns. If medication is making you feel like a zombie, then you're on the wrong medication or the wrong dose. Same answer for medications not helping. They might not completely correct the depression but the right medication regimen can improve your quality of life and mood, with few side effects or complications. If you're seeing a provider who keeps giving you the same medications that don't work, find a new provider. If it's because you're not telling the truth when you go see your prescriber, then come clean. Most people should expect a vast improvement in their mood and quality of life on the right medications with minimal side effects.

There are 2 situations that should lead you to consider taking medications. There is the person who is born with the genetic traits for depression that biologically need these drugs, and then there's the person who is going through a very difficult time in their life. Both of these situations should respond to medications. It does take more than medicine to become happy. Happiness also involves making healthy life choices, eating right, sleeping right, and exercising. It also involves being connected to others and feeling useful. There is more to happiness than just taking a pill. Your prescriber will help steer you in the direction of life changes that will improve your self-esteem and life quality. Often that is the role of therapy, and therapy is work. You can't expect to "get better" without making some life changes and working to improve your happiness, self-esteem, and life satisfaction. You have to work at it.

Some people are born to difficult life situations and some are just born with different biochemistry than others. It's not unusual to go through life depressed and not even be aware of it. A few years back a patient was referred to me because she took a screening tool for a medical procedure, and it indicated a very high level of depression. Although nothing about this woman's appearance or functioning suggested depression, when quantified using a validated professional testing tool, the level of depression was truly and extremely high!

How does that happen? First, we get conditioned to telling everyone we're "fine", which is just a meaningless pleasantry we exchange. Second, many of us believe feeling depressed indicates a flaw in our personality or emotions, so we don't tell anyone how we truly feel. Major depression is visible because it involves an acute change from how we usually feel and behave. But those who deal with daily and long standing chronic depression won't exhibit those changes in appetite, functioning, or appearance.

If you're one of those people, as I am, depression is a long standing struggle that can get better, but is often worse with stress. Having depression requires us to take extremely good care of our physical and mental health. It requires us to self-monitor because we can slip easily from struggle into darker and more dangerous thoughts. If this describes you, you need medication to correct your neurotransmitter imbalance so that most of the time you are experiencing some pleasure and quality to your life. There is danger to your health in not treating this as the medical condition it is. One is that, in response to external stressors, the balance to endure and live with that internal struggle can dip too low. In a full depressive period or in response to increased stress, the feat to keep functioning can feel insurmountable. I've come to the conclusion that depression is not unlike other mental illnesses in that it causes you to think and feel things that are not based in reality; you can feel things are too painful to endure, and that the pain won't end.

That's truly a mistake in your logic, because the events external to us do always change, but no one can convince you of that when you're in the midst of depression. You're the one who has to realize this is the cognitive equivalent of 'my brain is trying to kill me' **.

**Author's Note: A favorite quote from Jenny Lawson's, author of *Furiously Happy: A Funny Book About Horrible Things,* blog on Wordpress:

Mental illnesses like depression can be confusing.

While you would never argue with your doctor about treating your diabetes and taking medication, we often fight the idea to take medication to treat this disorder. But without treatment, your functioning is harder, your relationships are harder, and your health will suffer from the quiet internal stress you bear; eventually this will lead to other physical illness (gastric illness is most common). Often people are already experiencing these illnesses when they seek treatment for depression. Your medical doctor has to know about all health conditions.

They can provide an antidepressant, but a specialist in the field of psychiatry will be able to explain to you why the medication works a certain way and be better informed to provide the right medication to help your specific issues. Your brain is important to your overall health and functioning. It matters! A drug won't fix everything wrong in your life. You still have to do additional work to keep your brain healthy, and your life well. But don't add the burden of trying to forego medications if you've already been dealing with depression for a long time. Life is challenging enough already, take good care of yourself and get what you need for your health.

"Isn't suicide a sin?"

It is interesting that public opinion about suicide and the right of individuals to end their own lives varies throughout cultures and history. Today, only in the United States and India is it still considered to be a criminal offense. In a few states like Oregon, it has become decriminalized. In a popular media covered case, a young married woman with brain cancer moved to Oregon with her family to end her life with dignity, before the onset of severe debilitation could take place in her brain, and while she could make the decision rationally. In a movie, "Still Julia" the main character, a doctor diagnosed with Alzheimer's disease, leaves herself explicit instructions that she should be able to follow when that time came. If she hadn't of lost her cell phone with the secret instructions for as long as she had, she would have been successful.

Much of the Catholic Church regards suicide as a mortal sin in that it represents a denial of God and a denial of the gift of life. One of the 10 commandments clearly states that "Thou shall not kill" and this can literally be interpreted to mean oneself, but not every Christian sect supports that notion in the same black and white manner, and even fewer churches follow the edict that someone taking their own life should not be given a Christian burial. In the Jewish religion, there are historical references to numerous occasions where suicide was considered a form of Martyrdom, as when Saul fell on his sword (1020 B.C.) or when a whole community was succumbing to the Romans on the mountain of Massada (73 A.D.). The Lutheran Church in America does not consider suicide to be an unforgiveable sin. In Islam, suicide is considered a great sin, and is expressly forbidden in the Koran. "Suicide" terrorists are not strictly following the traditional Koran; they have redefined the Koran and part of a much smaller population of "extremist" Muslims who follow their own rules.

From my perspective, a deeply religious person who follows traditional beliefs about suicide being a mortal sin gives me a cushion to work from. These people who just don't believe that suicide is an option removes a lot of the risk that comes with treating people with major depression with suicidal thoughts, and I can concentrate more on their treatment and recovery.

"Most people who kill themselves have a mental illness"

Completely untrue. The majority of people who kill themselves have no history of mental illness. The majority of people who kill themselves do so for a variety of reasons, most commonly being told they have a terminal illness. They make the decision to spare themselves this painful and difficult decline. Of course, there are also many people who kill themselves because they are suffering from mental illness too.

"Children Never Suicide"

Children as young as 4 have tried to kill themselves, and children as young as 5 have completed suicide. A four year old was hospitalized locally after a suicide attempt. It is never too early to really try to understand what children around you are thinking.

Their friends might not know what's going on, but they might drop hints of what they're thinking. Parents and educators need to keep their eyes open. In the United States, each year about 30 children under 12 take their own lives.

Children are also most susceptible to copycat behavior. There are always copycat effects but if you're worried about someone who has had someone close to them suicide, you're right to worry. Suicide is a sudden traumatic loss, and when it happens to someone close, it can trigger a copycat behavior. Don't just worry about it, ask.

"Suicide can't be prevented because it's done on impulse" "They're just doing it for attention"

Also not true. The majority of people who suicide think about it for a long time before they attempt it. Impulsive gestures might be more common among the young, but are not less important and should be taken very seriously, as previous attempts often predict future completions. Many of the interventions to prevent suicide have had tremendous impact on reducing its occurrence. Removing firearm access, and many other interventions have been demonstrated to reduce incidence, which we will discuss more in the following chapter on prevention.

Chapter 3: Prevention

Don't ever underestimate the power or impact you can have on someone else's life. Someone contemplating suicide or experiencing severe depression isn't thinking logically, and you have to try to use every possible way to reach them, touch them, and let them know how important they are to you. You love them and are worried about losing them. People experiencing depression can be illogical, unable to think clearly and unable to take care of themselves. Sometimes even though you know they aren't doing well, you feel like you have no idea what you can do. This chapter is going to both try to answer that question, and give you information and resources so you feel less powerless.

Asking someone the question "are you thinking about ending your life" is an important question to ask those you're concerned about. If you're lucky, you'll get an answer or response like my son would give me; look at me in shock that I would even ask something so dumb. Another lucky response would be from those who consider suicide to be a mortal sin; those people won't take their lives because they won't go to heaven, because it strongly violates their religious codes. You can take a deep breath! You know now that you won't have to worry about them taking their lives. You still want to help them, and let them know you're there to help in any way you can. But many of us, at some time or another, will be so sad, or ashamed, or in so much pain that suicide will be something that will pass through our thoughts. It is very hard to admit this to someone else.

So if the first step in Prevention is to identify those who are at risk for suicide. How do you do this and evaluate how serious the risk is?

Evaluating Level of Risk

If a person close to you or that you know suddenly starts looking or acting differently, or they look sad or stop returning your calls, or if you just know they are depressed and your internal worry alarm is getting loud, ask how they are and listen to their voice. Share with them your concerns, share with them that they are important to you and that you're worried. Once they've admitted to you that they have some thoughts of wondering if life is even worth this pain, ask if they've thought of doing something to end it, and then ask how they would do it. I usually ask "have you thought about how you might do it?" Their answer tells you how serious they are and the level of danger in the current situation. If they answer something vague like "I'd probably take a train to New York and jump off the Empire States building", and they are in Nebraska, the answer is vague and lets you know the person isn't planning it at this present time, it's just a vague thought of wishing the current pain will end. The answer you get tells you the current level of risk. If there are active thoughts of suicide reported and the person has the means to carry this out along with access to the means, this is a medical emergency.

So for example, if the person contemplating suicide has access to a gun, and the person says they would shoot themselves, remove the gun and lock it up out of access, preferably out of the immediate household. If they refuse to let you take it, call 911. If their idea is to go into the garage and turn on the car and breathe in carbon monoxide, take away the car keys, and don't leave them alone. Whatever steps you can take to keep access from their selected means to carry out a suicide, the less urgent and less dangerous the situation becomes. Spend a few nights with them at their home or yours. Lock up their medications and yours. Get them access to a medical professional as fast as possible, and inform the professional. Involve other loved ones to be part of the safety plan. A mental health professional will likely not return your call unless it's a medical emergency, because of HIPPA protections, but often will if it's a life or death situation and you make this clear in your message. You cannot count on them and may decide to take your own action by calling 911, a crisis line, or suicide prevention hotline, any way you can get the person a good evaluation and connected to help as quickly as possible.

People get mad at family members who intervene this way, and might not share the truth in an emergency room, because they fear being hospitalized. Hospitalization is often not enough to prevent someone from suiciding the minute they get out, so if you can develop a safety plan you feel comfortable with, this is often a better option because it keeps the door of communication open between you and them. Many people intent on killing themselves can lie to the hospital staff to get released. It happens all the time.

A vague plan and vague thoughts of wishing to be dead are far less urgent than a person with a specific plan and access to those means. You have to intervene to prevent access to the means and prevent the person from being left alone if they are in this kind of danger.

If a person is actively suicidal and has access to the means, you may have to have them hospitalized. It is important you accompany them to the hospital, because if they get there and deny saying what they told you, they might be sent home with a doctor's appointment that might be 6 weeks or more away. It also takes medication close to 6 weeks to fully work, and working with a therapist to address their feelings and learn to handle them better also takes time. You want to make sure there's safety supports in place to keep them safe for some period of time in the meanwhile. You don't want them to be left alone if you're truly convinced there is risk they could act on their thoughts. So level of risk and the specificity of the plan and the access to the means are most important to determine. This should be evaluated anytime anyone makes suicidal statements or gestures such as cutting. This along with social withdrawal, sad mood, giving treasures away, phone calls out of the blue to multiple people telling them how much they are loved, or changes in interests or appetites are some of the warning signs of suicidal plans.

Notably, all cutting is not a suicidal gesture per se. Many young people use cutting as a tool to help relieve stress. It is however, a definite concern, and should be evaluated as a suicidal gesture- but if the cutting is away from the arteries and is a cut across the wrist rather than across the line of the artery, it is a gesture and this would not be considered an emergency requiring hospitalization unless the person is also stating the desire to die when they're cutting.

Many people cut as a coping strategy and are not cutting to try to kill themselves. This behavior requires attention but is dealt with using therapy to improve coping skills. Cutting is not necessarily a suicidal gesture, but a skilled professional needs to evaluate this to clarify the behavior and level of risk.

An excellent resource from the publication "Suicide Among Veterans and Other Americans 2001-2014", Office of Suicide Prevention expounds on this information. (Updated August 2017 by the Office of Mental Health and Suicide Prevention, US Department of Veterans Affairs.

1. Look for the warning signs

Presence of any of these warning signs requires immediate attention and referral. Consider hospitalization for safety until a complete assessment can be made.

- *Threatening to hurt or kill self*
- *Looking for ways to kill self*
- *Seeking access to pills, weapons, or other means*
- *Talking or writing about death, dying, or suicide.*

Additional Warning Signs
For any of the these signs, refer for mental health treatment or follow-up appointment.

- *Hopelessness*
- *Rage, anger, seeking revenge, acting recklessly or engaging in risky activities, seemingly without thinking.*
- *Feeling trapped—like there's no way out.*
- *Increasing alcohol or drug abuse.*

- *Withdrawing from friends, family, and society.*

- *Anxiety, agitation, inability to sleep, or sleeping all the time.*
- *Dramatic changes in mood.*
- *Perceiving no reason for living, no sense of purpose in life.*

2. Assess for specific factors that may increase or decrease risk for suicide

Factors that may increase risk:
- *Current ideation, intent, plan, access to means.*
- *Previous suicide attempt or attempts. Alcohol/substance abuse.*
- *Previous history of psychiatric diagnosis.*
- *Impulsiveness and poor self-control. Hopelessness—presence, duration, severity.*
- *Recent losses-physical, financial, personal.*
- *Recent discharge from an inpatient unit.*
- *Family history of suicide.*
- *History of abuse-physical, sexual, or emotional.*
- *Co-morbid health problems, especially a newly diagnosed problem or worsening symptoms.*
- *Age, gender, race-elderly or young adult, male, white, unmarried, living alone.*
- *Same-sex sexual orientation.*

Factors that may decrease risk:
- *Positive social support.*
- *Spirituality.*
- *Sense of responsibility to family.*
- *Children in the home, pregnancy.*

- *Life satisfaction.*
- *Reality testing ability.*
- *Positive coping skills.*
- *Positive problem-solving skills.*
- *Positive therapeutic relationship.*

3. Ask the questions
- *Are you feeling hopeless about the present/future?*

If yes, ask...
- *Have you had thoughts about taking your life?*

If yes, ask...
- *When did you have these thoughts, and do you have a plan to take your life?*
- *Have you ever had a suicide attempt?*

4. Responding to suicide risk
Ensure the patient's immediate safety and determine the most appropriate treatment setting. Refer for mental health treatment or ensure that a follow-up appointment is made.

Inform and involve someone close to the patient. Limit access to means of suicide. Increase contact and make a commitment to help the patient through the crisis. Provide the number of an ER/urgent care center to the patient and significant other.

How to Help Someone Contemplating Suicide

Anyone who knows a fellow human is struggling

should try to reach out to them and invite them to talk about what they are thinking, and to try to listen without judgment. When we hear of young people taking their lives we have to be careful how we approach discussion, trying to avoid judgmental comments that would scare our children from talking honestly to us. Contrary to common beliefs, asking someone if they are thinking of taking their life does not put that idea in someone's head-it invites them to actually talk about what they are thinking. I think many parents and teachers and family just get too afraid to ask, because they don't know what they will do if the answer is yes. But we really do need as a society to learn to ask this question of each other when we see each other struggling through hard times.

When I was first starting out working in psychiatry, one of my first volunteer jobs was manning a suicide hotline. It was an interesting and sometimes frightening job. But talking someone through and getting them to agree to speak with someone close to them and connecting them with someone who could help them was gratifying. These hotlines still do exist today, and exist in phone, text, and email formats.

Suicidal thoughts needs to be a subject we become comfortable discussion as suicide has become so rampant in our society. We have to get better at allowing people to feel okay about imperfect thoughts and feelings. We have to take the time to listen to each other, and be with each other. PUT THE ELECTRONICS DOWN!

We as a society save lives when we engage in true connections to others, without judgment as to their thoughts or conduct. We have to tell them no matter what they have to done or thought or how different they think they are, they are important and valuable.

People who are thinking about suicide are in a lot of emotional pain. While the pain could be a biological brain chemistry issue, it is more likely a response to overwhelming loss and frustration. Our culture places great emphasis on accomplishments and very little time is spent teaching our children how to deal with frustration and failure. At times, the most successful can be the most vulnerable when they encounter failure for the first time, or they just become exhausted by the constant strain to be "perfect." We are always the hardest in judging ourselves.

When people fail and feel frustrated, they are embarrassed and ashamed. How is it that we have taught our children that shame is the only appropriate response to failure? How can we evolve our society to praise the willingness to take a risk and educate ourselves that no success is ever achieved without failure? How can we encourage people to understand that failure is painful but also informative and valuable, and builds character? All successful people have endured failure at some point in their lives. Failure is as much a part of a successful life as any other quality. Somehow, we have to remind people of this more, and be less secretive and shameful over our own failures to those around us, especially those we care about.

It is also important to understand how to respond to those dealing with a difficult emotional time. We become fearful and may react to our fear. Do we fight? Do we take flight? Or do we freeze? There is an instinct in us that makes us want to back off when something scares us. People who are going through a difficult emotional time scares us. We become afraid we don't have the resources to help them, so we withdraw from them. We withdraw, they withdraw, and the more isolated they feel, the more likely they are to feel no one will care if they die. The most important thing you can do to prevent suicide is to ask the person you are concerned about what they're feeling. Ask directly if they have thought about taking their own life, or if they have thoughts of wishing they were dead. If they answer yes, you need to ask the next question- have they thought about how they might do it. If they give you a method of how, then they are actively thinking about it and your next step is to determine if they have access to that method and get them the appropriate help or devise a safety plan with them.

Did you know you can call the police to do a "well-being check" if you're concerned about someone's safety and they aren't returning your calls? The police will go to the home and talk to them. Usually these officers have been specially trained in doing this.

Your job as the confidant is to stay engaged and involved until and during the process where the person is engaged with a professional that will help them. Therapy and medications are important tools to be considered when someone feels that bad. Do your best to connect them with a professional, but don't underestimate the importance you have in their lives because they've told you what they're thinking.

So you've determined that someone you know and care about, or acting different than usual. They seem to act like the whole process of living is just exhausting and like they don't have the energy to do it anymore. They don't smile anymore and you're concerned if they're ok. What do you do?

You ask first if they are ok. You share that you have noticed they seem to be struggling more lately and you let them know you care. You try to get some answers about what's going on. You listen. Don't tell them what they need to do. Just listen to what's going on. Stay calm. You want them to feel safe enough with you to answer you truthfully.

Then you broach the difficult question like this, "Sometimes when people are going through a period like you are right now, it can feel like life is just too difficult. Have you ever had thoughts like that?" That can then lead to the next question, "Have you ever thought of acting on those thoughts?" If the answer is yes, the next question might be "Have you thought about how you would do it."

You're hearing them make comments like "I'm tired of feeling this way" "Life is just too painful", "I can't keep living like this" "I would rather die than go on living this way" "I just can't do this" are serious comments requiring your serious attention. Ask the person to explain what they mean. Ask if they are thinking about suicide. You find out they are thinking of ending their lives, what do you say next? The following few paragraphs could be paraphrased and give you some of the language to use in a discussion of this sort, something like this:

> "You matter to me. I don't think you know how much I need you. I would feel very lonely if I lost you. You are as

94

close to me as a _____ (father, brother,
sister etc). I feel the freedom to be
myself with you, whether good or bad. I
don't have that relationship with anyone
else that I have with you. I would be very
lost without you. I know it's hard for you
to think about right now, but I've seen you
come out of this before, I've even seen
you worse before, and I know you can
come through this again."

The above conversation is summary of some words that I said to a close friend of mine when she was going through a severe depression and contemplating suicide. When she did emerge from the depths of this, she told me that my words saved her life, and thanked me. When a person is in the midst of a major depressive episode, their mind plays an evil trick on them. It convinces them that they will never feel well again. It feels like the current depth of despair was never experienced before, even if it has. It convinces them that it will never go away and they will never feel better, even if they have been through it and recovered before. The pain is so great that it disturbs the mind's ability to reason.

That' is why it's incredibly important to convey to someone you know who is struggling, what impact they have on your life and how important it is for you to have them in it. Some of the paragraphs I have written below will hopefully give you a sense of how bad this feels when you're going through it, and hopefully offer up some language you can use when you're trying to convey your concerns to someone close to you.

"I know you are in a lot of pain, it feels like

nothing will ever get better. You feel like you are all alone in this horrible place, but please don't take your life. This really bad feeling feels worse because you think it will last forever. Maybe it went away for awhile and came back. Maybe something really painful orterrible has happened in your life and you feel it will never get better.

I understand it feels unbearable. It feels like you're dying, but you're not. You're just in pain and however bad it feels, it won't last forever and it will get better. I understand you don't know what to do. But don't give up. It's time for you to talk to someone you trust and tell the truth about what you're feeling so that we can help you. The most important thing to do right now is to try to calm yourself down. Sometimes a good night's sleep can make things look very different. Please stay away from alcohol and drugs right now. Those things affect your inhibitions and make you feel worse. Can I help you find help? Can you make me a promise to keep yourself safe? You are very important to me, I would be devastated if I lost you in my life. I need you.

Maybe we've forgotten to show you how important you are to us. Maybe we have been too distracted to show you how much we love you, or maybe it seems no one cares, but we do. We are out there. Many of us who work inthis field do so because it's important for us to help people like you, because we've been through it ourselves. We care about people and we care about you. We want to use everything we've learned to help you feel better and improve your life. As long as you don't give up, things will get better. Please tell us how much pain you are in and let us try to help.

Some of us have felt as badly as you're feeling right now. Some of have lost someone important to us to suicide, and we wonder every day what we could have done different to prevent it. The pain suicide causes to your loved ones will haunt them the rest of their lives. I know. I work with them every day. They had no idea your pain was this serious or that your despair was so great. They want to help you, if you talk to them you will find that out. We who work in this field want to help you. Please give us a chance.

Don't give up. It's time for you to talk to someone you trust and tell the truth about what has been going on. Don't give up. It's time for you to talk to someone you trust and tell the truth about what you're thinking so that we can try to help you. If you don't know who that is, then the Suicide Prevention Lifeline will help you identify who you can talk to. The most important thing to do right now is to try to calm yourself down. Pay attention to how you're talking to yourself right now; don't make yourself more scared by telling yourself it will never get better, because that's not true.

Those words are your depression talking, not you. Depression can fool your mind into thinking thoughts that aren't true, thoughts like something can never get better and that's just not the case. There's nothing bad about you for feeling this way, you just haven't had the opportunity to talk to someone who knows all about what it is you're going through. Lots of people have survived these kinds of episodes, and since one out of 10 people have, you already know someone who has survived just what you're going through right now. Just because someone you know has made you feel unlovable or sad, doesn't mean it will always feel this way. Just because someone else you know has given up doesn't mean you have to. It can take awhile to get better, but you have to get in touch with the people who can help you get through this. . I survived and got help from someone who helped me learn to like myself when I hated myself. You can survive this and feel better. Your life is valuable. Your survival will help a lot of other people

Whatever it is you're going through
right now is something you can survive
and you need to believe this is possible."

Letter to those who've been lost to suicide-
and the pain it leaves forever.....

Dear....,

"I wish I could have told you this...

*I will never know why I didn't know that it
was the last time I would ever talk to you.*

*I will never know why my love wasn't
enough for you to stay alive or why you
didn't give me the chance to show you it
was*

*I wish I could go back in time and figure
out the magic words I could have said to
stop you. I will blame myself for the rest of
my life because I have failed you.*

*You made a decision that would deprive
me of your love for the rest of my life.
The hole I feel now is a piece of what
you must have been feeling, but it just
makes me yearn for you.*

It's a hole no one could fill but you How

*could you give up before you even had a
chance to know what you would be
missing?*

You are gone but my relationship with you remains very much alive. I play the record over and over, wanting the ending to change and it never does.   I want to give you everything you need so you know you are valued and your place on this earth can feel a little better.   I want to help you get through this dark shadow and survive to the point where you can see the light again.   I want to do everything I can to help you and I want you to give me another chance. " **

**Authors Note: I found parts of that letter online, parts were from a survivor, and I wrote only parts of it. I searched online to find the original source, but couldn't find it. I apologize for failing to acknowledge the original author's words. I felt the words this letter conveys would be meaningful to someone contemplating suicide and wanted to include them.

I always make sure to tell everyone on every occasion I encounter who is thinking of suicide, how it will affect me personally. I have had a number of patients and friends tell me later, those words of how it will impact me, is one thing that kept them alive. *A person contemplating suicide is in the midst of their own personal hell and can't see very well outside themselves. Letting that person know how important they are to you and how much you will be hurt by their loss is a one of the most powerful things you can do to stop someone from carrying out their thoughts. Your words are powerful. Use them.

Why "What can I do to help?" Or "Is there Something I can do?" could be a useless question

When we are confronted in our daily lives by those who we see suffering, especially during a tragedy or what feels like one to them, we want to help. We often say to the person "What can I do to help?" and that's a beautiful question to ask except for one thing. The person who is despondent in their sadness is unable to think of anything. They might be bombarded by kind and well-meaning people who keep offering such comments. But truly, when we are in the midst of this kind of sadness and shock, the hardest thing we could do would be to ask someone for something helpful. Think of the last time you were really suffering. Very kind and loving friends may have spoken those same words, and they are kind words. But the person in pain is unable to even think of anything that could be helpful. They are immersed in their sadness. So if you really mean what you say when you speak those words, it would likely be even more helpful to offer something specific.

Here might be some examples of what you might offer or do:

> 1. Could I drop over a dinner? Could I order you pizzas tonight? The person might have no appetite but when the food is in front of them, they might be tempted. Or drop off some freshly baked cookies. Or a dried fruit and nut tray or basket. That way you know it doesn't have to be eaten right away.

2. Could I come over tonight and just answer your phones for you? Or are there any calls you'd like me to make for you?

3. Send anything. Sending flowers from a flower delivery service can be crazy expensive, but I can go to Home Depot or Costco and buy a beautiful Orchid plant for $20 that would cost me $75 to send from a florist. Just drop it off at the house. (sorry florists). It gets you inside to see how they really are.

4. What about sharing a favorite book, especially if one you have read and are passing on that helped you through a hard time? Maybe include a note about what you found most helpful, or mark pages with "this section really connected for me, I hope it helps you heal." This is an inexpensive and very thoughtful thing to do for someone in pain.

5. Could I come over and help you compile a list of thank you notes you want to write later? Or could I come over and help you write or address them? A favorite memory I have is of my grandmother, she wrote New Year"s notes every year and because she didn't write well, she had me write them for her. Sometimes I would help make suggestions of what to write or how to say it. The last thing anyone dealing with grief wants to do is

write those thank you notes. What a kind offer that would be!

Perhaps you can come up with other things you may have done, or that someone has done for you when you have dealt with trying times. The kindnesses, the way we reach out and help each other through such times can be truly healing. Be careful of the words you use, so you don't cause more pain for the person. Try to avoid platitudes or comments involving religious beliefs the person may not share with you. Try to be more thoughtful about who it is you are talking to. If you don't really feel like offering any help, then don't just say "is there something I can do?" If you really are only offering your acknowledge of their sadness, say so. Say "I'm sorry for your loss, I know this is a very hard time and very difficult for you" and stop at that. Think before you speak. Some very painful moments occur when people think they're helping but actually cause more hurt.

How to Help Prevent Suicide

People who are thinking about suicide are in a lot of emotional pain. The pain could be a biological brain chemistry issue, but more likely it is a response to overwhelming loss and frustration. We pride ourselves on accomplishments and very little time is spent teaching us to deal with frustration and failure. At times, the most successful can be the most vulnerable when they encounter failure for the first time. Other times, it is because of repeated failures.

When people fail and feel frustrated, they are embarrassed and ashamed. How is it that we have somehow learned that shame is appropriate when we fail? How can we evolve our society to praise the willingness to take a risk? How can we get people to understand that failure is hard but teaches you a lot and builds character? We have to start conveying to each other that failure is not the end of the world. All successful people have endured failure at some point in their lives. Failure is as much a part of a successful life as any other quality. Somehow, we have to remind people of this more, especially when people are overwhelmed and upset.

Your job as the confidant is to stay engaged and involved until and while the person is engaged with a professional that will help them. Therapy and medications are important tools to be considered when someone feels that bad. Do your best to connect them with a professional, but don't underestimate the importance you have in their lives because they've told you what they're thinking. Sometimes a good night's sleep can make things look and feel very different. Sometimes they just have to calm down by doing breathing and mindfulness exercises, do some together. Request they stay away from alcohol and drugs right now. Those things affect their inhibitions and can make them more likely to do something everyone will regret. Can you help them find help? Can you ask for a promise to keep themselves safe? Say "You are very important to me, I would be devastated if I lost you in my life. I need you."

The Role of Shame in Substance and Drug Abuse

Many people who develop substance abuse problems became that way when they tried to numb their feelings of intense pain. Most have a genetic predisposition to addiction that makes dealing with substances much more dangerous than what occurs when the rest of us dabble with use or overuse of substances.

That does not make you a bad person if that has happened to you. No one who hasn't been through this understands how difficult of a process it is to get sober. It is not easy and usually takes multiple attempts to be successful. Failing at something over and over again doesn't make your life or you unworthy or unlovable. You are loveable. Many people love you who want you to succeed at this, even if they have turned their backs on you because of past failures. They are just waiting to bring you into the fold of life again. Don't give up. Keep trying. Every day is a new day. All of them will welcome you back or others will take their place. Others who have recovered understand the pain you have gone through and the incredible effort it takes to survive that. Surround yourself and seek out those who understand

If you love someone who is currently trying to get sober, it is an exhausting and long process. It is hard to know how long to hope and hold on and when to let go. It is not the person you hate, it's the disease. It takes a lot of strength and support for you to keep this clear. You will also need help and support. Get involved with Alanon to help you sort out this process and get yourself support.

Sometimes you may need to temporarily let go of the relationship, if so you will have to have help to forgive yourself and forgive the person who has put you through this trial. Any way you look at it, it is not a black and white situation, stay away from others who think it is; they don't understand. People want clear black and white solutions which is not possible under these circumstances. Those close to you are likely not to understand. No one chooses to be in the painful throes of an addiction, and despite their desire to change, it's extremely difficult. You will need to get support so you can tolerate this process.

A vast number of people who die from their addictions, do so because of the extreme shame of a relapse. The idea of going through the process of getting sober again is so disheartening, so overwhelming, that they "accidently" overdose. Make sure they know you're there for them, no matter how many times it takes, or how many mistakes they make, and that you'll be waiting.

Chapter 4 Suicide Prevention: Teaching Coping Skills and Self-Calming Strategies

You might be of the belief that the family you are born into, and what opportunities you receive, determines your quality of life and success in it. Certainly, both can be life advantages but are no guarantee whatsoever about life quality and happiness. This chapter, probably the most important, will introduce you to a variety of proven techniques to improve life quality and happiness. As you read through each section, you will see some reoccurring themes with much overlap. Each of these techniques were developed by different people and were not meant to be exclusive. All of these methods are teachable, which means you can focus on any of them to improve your life.

When you look at the people society admires most in the world, it is usually those who have created their own success and happiness, and not those who have had it handed to them. We admire those who have overcome adversity. We also admire those who choose to do something for the world with their success, rather than simply use their success for their own power or gain.

Even though you can't control the family or circumstances you were born into, you can still change your life. Although I have never discussed this out loud before, I can tell you that for most of my life, I was not a very likable person and I had no idea why. I had issues maintaining relationships and people drifted out of my life and I had no clue why. At some point in my young life, I realized that no one wanted to be with me and I knew that it must be something I was doing or some way I was behaving that repelled people. I knew I had to make a decision to change and I started watching how successful people socialized.

In my social life, I realized I often quickly spoke out in groups and said things others were thinking, so initially people identified me as a leader. Sometimes I quickly became in charge in groups. However, being identified as a leader causes more eyes to be on you, and people in charge are often not well liked because like me, they have no idea how to handle that power. I had very poor people skills.

Once all of my flaws became visible, the power I assumed I had was quickly lost and faded to embarrassment and avoidance. I always tell my patients that every mistake you make will occur again, and provide an opportunity to learn to try something different, because all of our failures repeat themselves. The person who always embarrasses you will try to do it again, so you'll have another opportunity to handle it differently the next time. Eventually I learned that when in a group, when too many eyes began looking at me and asking what I thought, I learned to throw the focus to someone else's thoughts, and in this way avoided taking on a social role I knew I could not manage successfully. I would visibly watch the looks of disappointment register on people's face as I did it, but I succeeded at avoiding a commitment I knew would disappoint many more if I took it on.

In personal relationships, I often monopolized conversations. At some point, I realized that it is important to ask questions in my interactions. I found that successful connections in a personal relationship required actually listening to the answer to a question without interruption. Validation is vitally important to self-esteem, and validating a person's feelings is one of the biggest gifts you can provide another human being. If you are lucky, you have a few people who do this for you. If you don't, find those who can provide valuable interaction and validation.

This is something you need to search for. I watched what people with many friends did, and I emulated that to the best of my ability. Luckily, I became better with practice and now enjoy more meaningful relationships.

When I first studied psychology in the 1970s, the focus of study was psychopathology. Psychology has evolved significantly since then, exploring the factors that go into developing resourceful and successful living, despite what situations people were born into. Much of success and happiness in life is based on the personal narrative one tells oneself about that situation. Methods that can be studied and learned can foster healthy and happy lives. This chapter will be introducing you to a few powerful ones, and I hope will offer you the opportunity to further explore those you find most helpful.

What you will find here are a variety of clinically

proven and useful techniques to improve how you think, how you function, and how you feel. This chapter is intended as an introduction to teachable methods to improve mental health and quality of life. Any one of these topics has multiple books devoted to it for further study, and this is intended to introduce you to some of my favorites. Hopefully, each person who pursues this chapter needing help dealing with life will find something useful that can help you cope and recover from life's challenges

Cognitive Behavioral Therapy (CBT)

Our brain doesn't know the difference between what's real and what we imagine. We often experience what we expect to because we behave in a way that supports it. We can use that to our advantage – example being Matthew Sanford, the yoga instructor who was paralyzed from the chest down as a teen. He learned and practices yoga since his injury. His muscle tone in the affected areas continues to be stronger and better toned than others with the same condition. His brain is still making the connections, so there is benefit to his practice. Even though he can't control his extremities, the muscles are still responding to the thoughts in his brain. And that means this:

When you say bad things to yourself over and over, it has an impact.

Whatever we practice gets stronger- so the solution is to practice being kind and loving to ourselves. We all make mistakes. Mistakes are necessary for us to learn things. The discomfort helps motivate ourselves to change for the better. If you react to a mistake by beating yourself up more, adding to that mistake, the only thing that changes is how you feel about yourself.

In my previous book on relationships, I emphasized that if we always start from the premise that each of us are doing the best we can and as much as we can, then we can more readily understand and forgive others' mistakes. Taking others' behavior personally, causes us to talk about the offense to others, harbor on the negative, and stay in a place of anger and hurt. While that may not feel very good, many of us choose anger over sadness because anger feels more comfortable. Anger makes us feel strong. Sadness makes us feel vulnerable. Anger is a feeling of power and strength. Sadness is a place of letting go and acknowledging our powerlessness. There is no life without loss and sadness, and we have to get okay with dealing with those feelings. If you spend too much time trying to avoid those feelings because they are painful, they stay there. When you stop pushing those feelings away and we permit ourselves to feel the pain and then survive that pain, the pain begins to weaken. We have to get more comfortable with our difficult feelings by honestly embracing them when they occur, to allow ourselves to heal.

If you persist in pushing the feelings away, the pain may linger. Think of taking a volleyball and pushing in down in a swimming pool. It takes effort to keep pushing it down but pushing it down doesn't make it go away, it stays there – bobbing up to the surface. Healing begins when you learn to let it go and let yourself just feel the feelings. While it can be very uncomfortable, that severe level of discomfort eventually passes in less time than you expect. That happens because we adjust to even the worst situations with time.

Cognitive Behavioral Therapy's (CBT) roots came out of developments of early psychiatric studies from the 1800s, when Pavlov began studying behavioral modification techniques. The basic premise was that behavior can both be taught and modified with training and reward. Beginning in the early 1900s, these trainings and studies began to look at applications in human behavior. In the 1950s, the first popular approach and application was introduced in Norman Vincent Peale's "How to Make Friends and Influence People" which introduced the concept to the populace that it wasn't necessarily what people did that influenced outcomes but how they appeared to feel and think that did. Behaving in a successful way resulted in success and more likeability outcomes. One could pretend to feel confident and successful and this led to actual success.

The notion that behaviors may be learned grew into the observed premise that what you think affects your behavior. The quality of your relationships and choices are driven by what you think. You can learn to think differently and this will not only change your behavior, but also your relationships, and your thoughts about yourself. CBT grew out of this and other studies, and remains the premise of most psychotherapy done today. Through therapy, people are taught to identify their dysfunctional thought processes and change them. Based on the 1960s book by Dr. Aaron Beck "Cognitive Behavioral Therapy" this process is widely used today and very successful.

I read "Feeling Good; The New Mood Therapy" by Dr. David Burns MD in 1980 and this book changed my life. I will attempt to explain this to you in the manner I understood from this book and other resources. I do not profess to an expert in CBT. I can only tell you that I began utilizing this approach in 1980 to address my depression, and that this approach has continued to be a daily practice in my life and one I use when I find myself upset or thinking bad or sad thoughts that are making me unhappy. Both Dr. Beck and Dr. Burns list a number of mistakes in thinking that can lead us to feeling bad, so the first step is to examine your thoughts and consider how to correct your thinking.

Much of what makes us feel depressed are our own negative thoughts. Often we internalize negative thinking as a result of previous interactions with others, and don't even realize we are doing it. We continue to torture ourselves with the same critical or mistaken thought processes that made us feel powerless, unhappy, and resentful as children.

Consider what happens when you go to a movie. Perhaps you are in the mood for a comedy. You are expecting and preparing for entertainment to make you laugh. If you've picked well, you will go there and laugh and your expectations will be met. This will support your expectations and you will leave happy. Likewise, if you choose an interesting drama or thriller, you search for what you're expecting. The same thing is what happens with our thoughts. Our thoughts are like an internal movie script that dictates our behaviors and feelings. If you're always in a depressing critical thought pattern, you will always be feeling sad and upset with yourself and others. You then program and base your day based on these negative expectations, and what you do often proves you true. The only way to correct this is to correct your thought processes.

It takes work to change your thinking. Just wanting to do it won't make it happen. Anything worth getting good at is going to require some knowledge and practice. Other people telling you you're smart or attractive or good at something won't work if you constantly tell yourself the opposite. So you have to practice which will take time and effort.

Let's begin with some of the common faulty thoughts processes as categorized by Dr. Beck and Dr. Burns and begin to identify which of these sound familiar.

1. "All or Nothing Thinking" This pertains to thinking about your experiences in extreme positive or negative terms. You fail at one effort, so that means you are a failure. Everything is black and white, good or bad. Perfect or failure. What incredible pressure you have created for you. I sometimes give my perfectionistic patients an assignment to make a choice to purposefully do something half way, do just a good enough job on purpose. They usually laugh at me for even suggesting such a thing, and wonder why their anxiety is so constantly high. These same people have no issues accepting imperfection in others, it is only they themselves that they hold to this impossible standard

Close in association to all or nothing thinking, is -

2. "Over-generalization" This occurs when you believe that because one bad thing happened one time, it will happen every time. A man gets rejected when he asks a woman on a date, or maybe this happens two or three times. *An optimist with a clear sense of self* and positive goal mindset puts those failures behind them and keeps trying. The person who over-generalizes quits trying and never tries again. The salesman who gets rejected looks for another line of work. The little girl who falls off her bike concludes she can't ride and refuses to try again. Over-generalizing from one bad experience results in expectations of failure, and since what we expect affects our behavior, results in more failure, becoming a doomed life cycle of disappointment.

3. "Mental Filter" refers to the focus on one thing to the exclusion of everything else. It refers to focusing exclusively on one aspect of a situation and seeing the rest through this distorted filter. This is what happens when you look in the mirror and see one body area you're unhappy with so you think "I'm ugly." This kind of thinking means you always feel bad about yourself, because no human isever perfect in every part of their life, or their appearance. Some models and actors have been wildly successful who have been told they're too fat (Rebel Wilson, Ashley Graham), they have an imperfection or gap between teeth (Lauren Hutton) or a mole that should be removed (Cindy Crawford). Instead of taking that advice, they pursued their goals in spite of their imperfections, and became known for them. If they had bought into that all or nothing thinking or advice, they would have never been as successful as they became. They had to overcome stereotypes and believe in themselves to become the successful.

4. "Disqualifying the Positive" This is when the mind gets so conditioned to expecting negative because of practicing negative thinking for so long, that without realizing it, you turn every positive event *into something negative. Something good happens to* you, and you begin to feel anxious because 'you know' it will be followed by something bad. Someone gives you a compliment, like "your hair looks so nice" and you respond with "yes, I really shouldn't neglect it as much as I do, I'm so lazy." You disqualify anything positive or negative that happens. This constant negative framing of whatever happens to you leads to depression. You expect the worst, and you project that and get the worst. I remember going out with an extraordinarily handsome young man when I was in my early 20s. I kept wondering what he could possibly see in me. I also lived with an extremely beautiful roommate with little moral character. It was just a matter of time until I caught them together. But did I drive them to it? I certainly put the idea in their heads enough times which couldn't have helped. By constantly negating our relationship, and constantly repeating that I didn't understand why he was with me, I certainly set the stage. I expected it, and life has a way of manifesting what we expect.

5. "Jumping to conclusions" You see something and automatically conclude that something bad is happening. Let's say you're on a group or family trip. Because you are not part of that conversation, you see the others talking softly and laughing and assume they're laughing at you. Or that they prefer to be without you and have more fun without you, so next time you're invited to participate in an activity, you decline. Then you watch them enjoying that activity and conclude you were right, they didn't want you to begin with. You jump to negative conclusions and as a result, act in a fashion that supports those conclusions, sometimes causing your own exclusion. After you turn down the invitations a few times, they quit asking. Then you're all alone and no longer invited, and you wonder what happened. So finally you ask why you never get invited, and by now you're upset and accusatory. You confront them with "you never include me, you're so mean to me" and then you're even more isolated and lonely. You read their mind, and foretell the future in a negative way. This kind of thinking happens often with panic attacks. A person experiences some unusual sensations in their body when they're feeling very stressed. They jump to the conclusion that they're having a heart attack and run to doctors, ERs and specialists. They are sure they are dying, and that the doctors and tests can't find the problem. Eventually, thousands of dollars and tests later, no physical issue is found and the doctor sends them to see a psychiatrist for medication to prevent the panic attacks. This extreme catastrophic thinking and "fortune telling" makes the stress and anxiety much worse, and now there are thousands of dollars in medical bills to deal with as well. Even patients I am well established with have gone through this process during especially hard times. They talk themselves in being just as afraid of the medications as they are about dying. It's literally crippling.

6. "Magnification and Minimization" You make the mistake in your thinking of either blowing things up and magnifying them to be enormous, or shrinking them down to being nothing. The boss calls you into their office and tells you they want to speak with you. You walk in shaking, thinking this is it, you've made that fatal mistake and are about to be fired. A lot of us walk around with a constant feeling of dread, that we're a fake and it will be discovered how false and awful and inadequate we are. We walk around with a feeling of dread, just waiting for the next bad thing to happen because we expect it. A lay off at work, even when it involves a lot of people, you're just sure it *happened to you because of you. You magnify all of your imperfections, and you minimize all of your good*

118

qualities. Either way, you're setting yourself up for rejection and pain.

7. "Emotional Reasoning" occurs when you interpret your emotions as facts and generalize about them. Let's say I am a woman who is very self- conscious about her weight. I have a party to go to and I have gained five pounds. To most observers, five pounds is unnoticeable, but I convince myself I look horrible, so I dress in a way that displays how huge I feel, wearing something loose and baggy and not at all flattering. No one makes a comment on how I appear, because I don't look very nice, so I conclude they are all looking at me and thinking about how bad and fat I look. You go to a job interview. You're already feeling like a failure for losing your last job and feeling like you're a big loser. What do you think happens on the next job interview?

8. "Personalization" occurs when we ascribe everything around us to be based on something we did, said, or are. For example, we could see people around us who might be busy, distracted, or feeling unwell but we interpret this personally as that we are ugly, distasteful, being avoided, etc. We interpret the world and what happens as being a reflection of our own dysfunction and self- loathing, when what happens around us might have nothing to do with us.

9. "Fortune Telling, Catastrophic Thinking:" We expect disaster to strike at any moment. Any time something good happens means that something far worse is about to befall you. So you quit before you start. Why even try? Or when you hear of something bad happening to someone else, you immediately begin obsessing about it happening to you and obsess about how to avoid it.

10. "Blame" We blame the outside or others for everything bad that happens to us, believing that the control for our happiness is not ours, and that we're helpless to change it.

11."Should, Rightness, and Fairness" There are a multitude of situations we encounter growing up where we're taught this idea of fairness. It's so illogical! It works with children, but adult life is anything but fair! People get opportunities and get promotions based on who they know, and what connections they have. Merit doesn't always get success, nor does talent. It can be very confusing! Fairness has little to do with how things go sometimes. It is irrational thinking to expect that everything should be fair. "Should" is an irrelevant. You have to deal with what is. Should only results in faulty expectations. "Shoulds" are this list of rules we've learned about how everything "should" function but rarely does. Parents have intractable rules that are taught to follow in order for there to be some sense of order in the home. But every home has a different set of rules. Does this mean your home is right and everyone else's home is wrong? Rules set you up to expect life to be predictable. Life is not predictable. You want to be able to expect others to do the right thing, but you might not agree as to what the right thing is. So you become angry, because you expect them to know what you expected. You need to have realistic notions and be flexible and be able to adapt to be healthy. No one is ever always right. There's always multiple perspectives to every problem. Wars are fought over who is wrong and who is right, when rightness is much less important than *peace.* "Shoulds", when applied to ourselves or others result in anger and resentment.

12. "Magical Thinking" Everyone loves fairy tales. I love the idea of karma. Sometimes criminals eventually do get caught and punished, and bad people end up alone. I love the idea that the world is somehow keeping score and that eventually everyone's hard work will be recognized and rewarded. That you'll end up with God in Heaven for all the good you've done and the sacrifices you have made. If that is your logic for being a martyr, I hope you find that heaven. But meanwhile, back down on earth, you often have to make a point to take credit for your contributions to sure they are noted and rewarded. Once in a while a talented "wait staff" gets discovered and becomes a Hollywood star, but don't put all of your eggs in that basket. Most of us have to work good and hard while pointing out our contributions in order to get our just rewards.

You can see that there is a lot of overlap, or perhaps my explanations seem that way, but the message of CBT is that you have faulty thought processes and you
need to work to change them.

It works like this. After you've identified your dysfunctional thought process, you work to retrain your thoughts to be more logical and rational. Like anything worth getting good at, this requires a lot of time, practice and patience. You journal your thoughts, so you can read back on the unhealthy thought processes and reframe them when you calm down. You can choose a more logical and healthy response to replace that negative thinking, so that the that the next time you think that same negative thought, you are ready with a more rational response to replace it. Here's where having the journal to refer

to is so helpful. You don't have to worry about
forgetting what you've learned, because you will.
You will get lazy and revert back to negative thought
processes without practice, because those negative
thoughts were previously programmed. But now
when you find yourself feeling bad or mad, ask
yourself why? What cognitive distortions are you
doing? Can you say something different to change
them? Yes! And will that change how you feel? Of
course it will. You'll go back to your journal and it
will be easier to practice thinking healthier.

Prepare yourself a journal and start making notes
about the unhappy, angry or critical thoughts you're
having. At the moment you're experiencing them, you
might not be able to analyze what's irrational about
them, but at least write down what they are. Make
yourself a workbook. It could be a cheap spiral
notebook of any kind.

This is an example of what you should set up.
Have a column for your negative thoughts, how those
thoughts make you feel, what Mental Distortion
you're using, and what a Rational Response would be
as in the following examples:

Negative Thoughts	How I feel	Mental Distortions	Rational Response
I don't want to go to the party. I won't know anyone there. I'll be sitting by myself, feeling like a loser.	Scared, scared of being alone, Afraid of being judged by others as unwanted and as	Personalization, Catastrophic Thinking, All or Nothing Thinking	I know I am afraid of going to this party and not knowing anyone there; but, since no one knows me, they also won't know if I'm a loser or a successful

	unlovable as I feel		person. It's good for me to try new things. It always helps me grow to face my fears. I can park by the snacks and ask people how they know the host.
I hate all the people at this job. No one ever is respectful of me or likes me. Why would anyone else hire me? I'm such a loser.	Stuck, sad, self-hateful	Personalization, Emotional Reasoning, Disqualifying the Positive	I can prepare my resume and send it out. There are lots of people looks for jobs right now, but eventually I'll get an interview. It helps me feel more positive to know I'm trying. I will never know what could be different if I don't try changing it. Just thinking about doing that makes me feel better.
Jaime broke up with me and Jaime was my last shot at love. I will never find love. I will always be alone. No one will ever want me. I'm not lovable. I can't live alone, I might as well kill myself.	Sad, self-hateful, unlovable	Overgeneralizatio n, Catastrophic Thinking, Emotional Thinking, Magnification	It's appropriate and okay to feel sad right now- I've lost a valued relationship. I have to let myself feel this pain and learn from this experience. There's nothing I can do, but allow myself to feel these bad

			feelings. I will be kind to myself and let myself have the time I need to cry and rest in order to heal. This even does not predict what will happen in my future. I can find a happy, healthy relationship someday. It's silly of me to think suicide is a solution to this. I will never have the chance to find and feel happiness if I give up.

Change is as simple as buying a journal and beginning to monitor your thoughts and work to change them. Practice saying the positive thought to yourself. See if you can notice the next time something similar happens and you find yourself feeling bad, to repeat the positive thoughts and practice incorporating these into your daily life.

Teaching Resiliency

The American Psychological Association defines resilience as, "the process of adapting well in the face of adversity, to trauma, tragedy, or threats or significant sources of stress - such as family and relationship problems, serious health problems or workplace and financial stressors." Like other skills, the ability to handle stress is something that can be taught, developed, and strengthened. This section will delve into the information about how to improve your ability to handle stresses and recover from them quicker. Inherent in this ability to cope is your personal narrative, whether you see yourself as in control of your life and circumstances or whether you believe your happiness is at the whim of what the world sets at your door. It is incredibly important to feel you are in control, and a number of factors go into developing this perspective.

When two people experience the same stressors, how they handle them is a reflection of their personal narrative. An example would be how two different people respond to a loss of a child. One parent might go into a deep personal depression along with drug and alcohol abuse, while another might get involved in some way to try to prevent that tragedy from affecting another parent. If you feel you have no control over life and that it is just painful, you become depressed. If you feel you have some control, you activate to try to do something and take the sad event to mobilize and reframe your life narrative to feel you can improve something for others. The second choice activates you and connects you to others, reconnects you to life and increases your sense of purpose.

With all the stress involved in the world today, with all the terrible events that happen far too often, it is more important than ever to develop coping and resiliency skills. The time to develop these skills is before we need them. Having a loving and caring support system is extremely important. But probably half of us grow up without those types of parents, which makes resiliency harder to achieve. Again, personal narrative comes into play. If the issues at home cause a young person to conclude that adults aren't safe, aren't trustworthy, and that they are unlovable, they are far more likely to feel despondent and consider suicide. If those issues are interpreted instead with the narrative "I can't wait to
grow up and get out of here and then I'll live a life that will make me happy," the narrative changes to their being in control of changing the things in their life that they can, and the belief that they can make those changes which will make them happier in the future. Having that goal to survive and surmount these hardship is what makes the difference.

The development of resiliency includes developing the understanding that all life requires courage, and joy as well as pain, and it is important to experience all of it. Forgiveness has to be cultivated for those who have caused you pain for you to heal from it.

Finding a sense of purpose, your own search for meaning, is important to enduring all you have to in order to flourish. It helps keep you from giving up. Having a meaningful goal and feeling like you is contributing to the world is important. Being a nice person and helping others around you can be a good start.

How do you know if you need to develop your resiliency?

Answer this question; what is your response and internal dialogue when things feel out of control? Do you feel confident to handle what life throws in your path, or do you often find yourself thinking, "I just don't know how long I can go on this way?" Do you feel helpless when things go wrong in your life? Resiliency is what determines how you respond to stress. It is the capacity to respond to difficult times in a healthy and productive way. It is how you think about and cope with the difficulties in life that creates resiliency, and this skill can be developed and strengthened. There is an inherited part of this in our genetics. The most resilient people have the longest serotonin transport alleles in their brains, but despite your genetics, these skills can be developed and strengthened.

Resiliency research has looked at children from very high risk homes. These families experience poverty, divorce, mental illness, substance and other abuse. Yet a third to about half of the children who emerge from these homes thrive in spite of these difficult beginnings. What are the characteristics of these youngsters that helps them to thrive in spite of the odds? Why do two children from the same home turn out so differently? Studying those survivors and their characteristics has provided information about skills that can be intentionally developed.

Resilient people are hopeful and have realistic optimism. They have hope for the future. They have the ability to find the silver lining in most clouds. They believe they can overcome their adversity. This belief results in happier and healthier people who do better in life. Resiliency is about experiencing and problem solving best choices in difficult situations. It involves thinking in more accurate but also hopeful ways. When children and adults feel more confident that they have the ability to succeed, they do. Resiliency is about teaching these skills.

Emotional regulation involves the ability to feel in control of your emotions, attention, and behavior. People who have difficulty controlling these have a very difficult time maintaining relationships and employment. Emotions are contagious. Being around other angry or upset people increases your own level of upset and anger. Others who are trying to regulate their emotions stay away from those who are having difficulties controlling theirs because these people's lives seem full of chaos and drama. It's exhausting for others and threatens their own sense of ability to control their own functioning. The goal isn't the lack of emotional expression but control of it- the right time, the right amount, and at the right place.

Resiliency, as true in most areas of Positive Psychology, overlaps with many of the main concepts of CBT previously discussed, because it also drew on the work from Aaron Beck. This area notes the forms of problematic thinking as jumping to conclusions, tunnel vision, magnifying and minimizing, over-personalizing, externalizing too much, over-generalizing, mind reading, and emotional reasoning. It encourages those learning the process to be aware of your own thinking, your skills, and be aware of those thought patterns you need to change. They refer to these as "A-B-C" steps. "A" steps are recognizing Adversity, or what sets you off and makes you lose control. "B" refers to your belief system, the "ticker tape" of thoughts that begins running through your head when something (A) sets you off. "C" refers to the Consequences of those thoughts, your feelings and behavior once "A" occurs.

Understanding resiliency involves plugging these steps into situations and figuring out how your thoughts and behaviors can lead to more desirable consequences, improving sense of self control and satisfaction with yourself. Learning your A-B-Cs and how they interact is the first resiliency skill. The next step is to note your own problematic thinking and do your best to control and avoid these bad habits, but also to be more aware of which you seem to do most often. The third is recognizing icebergs, or deep underlying belief systems about how you feel the world ought to operate or how you feel you should operate within the world. It's also important to be aware of other people's icebergs as well, as they could be the source of the strain you feel in that relationship.

An alternative ABC step I've adapted, based on resiliency literature involves the concepts of emotions, attention and behavior. A = attention, what part of what is happening are you paying attention to? What are your thoughts about what you're focusing on? This is your B=belief system, and your belief system leads to your C=conduct. The first step in unraveling this reactive behavior that you seem to have no control over, is to use you're A=attention to focus on what you've been missing in the picture. What else is present, who else is present, and what else is happening or might be happening from the other person's perspective. Then you can begin to address your B- belief systems and examine, what other beliefs could be possible? What beliefs do the other parties possibly have? What beliefs might an uninvolved observer have looking at this situation? You begin to work on developing empathy skills by looking at other possible perspectives. Based on these different possible alternatives of what is occurring, can you now see that the variety of behaviors would vary based on what you believe is going on. When you've taken this step back, and examined it from various perspectives, your conduct is likely to change.

You get yourselves in trouble when you act without thinking, not paying attention to the processes that led to your conduct. You feel better when you feel in control. Look at your conduct and examine what beliefs and attention led to this conduct. Now choose the conduct you wish to emulate to get to your life goals. What belief systems support this healthier conduct? What kinds of things should you be paying attention to in order to change your negative belief systems, so that your conduct becomes one you feel in control of, and proud of?

Another area of skill development is learning to put the negative fears and thoughts into perspective. When you find yourself focused and consumed with worrying about something you fear, you can work to actually try to come up with a best-case scenario as well. You can begin to work towards the most likely consequence and with the improved calm that comes when you rid your thoughts of the catastrophe, and instead work on problem solving techniques to address and attend to the most likely scenario. Learning self-calming skills is vital to be able to look at your negative self-talk and approach your issues differently.

In summary, the essential elements of Resiliency training involve shifting the internal narrative to be one that involves the belief that you can change your life. You need to accept that you have the power to choose happiness, and make choices that support it. You need to understand that you have control over your thought processes and do the hard work to modify your internal dialogue. You need to focus on the key components of internal control of your attention, behavior, and conduct. Identifying your belief system, and self-calming enough to be able to see how it changes your emotions can be accomplished working with a skilled therapist. The therapist will help you understand the dynamics that contribute to your unhappiness. When you understand that you can change your life for the better, and that this is within your control the world becomes a different place. A skilled therapist helps you to accomplish this.

I came across a wonderful newsletter put out by The Family Institute at Northwestern University for parents who want to help their child transition back to school following a summer break. I felt the article said a lot about fostering resiliency and will share the highlights here, as I feel these are good areas for all human development. The article encourages parents to foster responsibility, brain development, resilience, self-esteem and humility. To foster responsibility, help your child become responsible in making decisions about their homework. Reminding them to do it, and if they don't, then let them feel the consequences of that. Let them approach it in their own way. For brain development, make sure there are periods of down time and relaxation, and that they have adequate sleep. No one makes good personal decisions when exhausted. Perhaps before a big test, some down time to watch a funny television and laugh. Help each child get enough rest and relaxation and make some of their own decisions about how time is spent. Resilience develops and increases each time you let a child make a decision and help them survive the consequences. Be supportive, but let them work out as many of their conflicts as possible. Help them develop their self-esteem by letting them do more for themselves and others, let them find the things they've lost, or forgotten. If they're constantly late, they can walk or ride their bikes if they miss the bus. They don't learn anything by you driving them there. Make sure they know you love them not only for their achievements but just for who they are, and that frustration is part of the process of learning, as is failure. Humility is learned by helping them understand that they're equally important as everyone else, and they need to adjust their needs to be respectful of others.

Here is a resiliency exercise I encourage my patients to do, although they often say this is "impossible." Try to do one new thing each day, or do something you do every day in a different way. This practice helps you expand your flexibility and often leads to new insights.

Mindfulness and Happiness

I thought it was astounding when someone commented on a class I was teaching on happiness by asking: "Why? Is happiness so hard to come by?" she asked. What a lucky person she must be! For many of us, happiness is something we seek and seems impossible. If happiness was so easy, most of the major philosophers would not have spent so much time discussing what comprises it. Many of us need to make some effort to find and keep a happy outlook.

The University of California Berkeley offers a free class called "The Science of Happiness" available on the site "EdX." The moderators Drs. Emiliana Simon-Thomas and Dacher Keltner discuss research on "Happiness" and what comprises it, as well as habits you can cultivate to increase the amount of happiness in your life. A ratio of three positive thoughts to one negative thought creates a mental state of happiness. Most of us manage two positive thoughts for every one negative we think. People who are depressed are closer to a one to one ratio. So one of the things that you can do to become happier is to monitor your thinking and if you find yourself thinking negatively, you can counter that by thinking positive thoughts. Activities such as making gratitude lists and taking the time to think of all the things that are wonderful in your life is a way to start focusing yourself on the good things that you have.

For some reason, when you just let your mind wander, you end up thinking 67% negative thoughts. That's the ratio that causes depression. When your minds wanders, you mostly wander to unhealthy thoughts, and those unhealthy thoughts make you feel depressed. The reason that activities like yoga and Tai Chi improve health and happiness is that they are activities that quiet your brain and make you focus on the present moment. When you practice either of these activities or similar things that involve your whole attention, you notice you feel happier. Yoga is actually a physical practice that was designed for physical and mental health.

The poses are intentionally difficult in order to put you in a mind state that requires your full attention in order to attempt them. It is not the perfect pose that is the purpose, but the process of trying. By placing your full attention on that effort, while trying to maintain breathing, you turn off all other thoughts. During that process you are practicing "Mindfulness," so that at the end of class, you have turned off the wandering thoughts or as it is referred to in yoga, the "monkey" brain.

Unhealthy thoughts such as predicting your future as catastrophic or hopeless lead you to feeling unmotivated today. Thinking everything is black or white, or that there is only one right way to do things limits your creativity and others' as well. Harsh self-judgment or harsh judgment of others fills your mind with anger and makes you feel irritable. Having expectations increases your sense of disappointment. The belief that you are powerless over your life or that it's unfair, is both untrue and inaccurate. The harder you try to control what can't be controlled, the more frustrated you will feel. What you can control is yourself and your thoughts. Even when you're doing something you don't like, you will feel happier focusing on it than daydreaming. You're going to be healthier if you pay attention to what you're doing in the present moment rather than letting your thoughts drift off. Practicing mindfulness is the way to fix this.

Jon Kabat-Zinn is the person who coined the practice and the term "Mindfulness." He says "as long as you're breathing, there's more right with you than wrong with you so we're going to pour more energy into what's right with you and then let the rest take care of itself....mindfulness is about living your life as if it really mattered, moment by moment by moment." "Mindfulness" is a modified form of meditation. Instead of trying to clear one's mind completely of all thoughts as is done in traditional meditation, "Mindfulness" practice encourages complete attention on one single thing in the present moment.

Mindfulness practice is used in the medical treatment of many conditions at the University of Massachusetts Medical School and Hospital where he is affiliated. Patients who elect to participate in the training have faster levels of recovery from cancer, heart surgery, and other illnesses, as well as reduced incidence of depression.

"Mindfulness" is a cultivated mental state that focuses you on the present, the here and now, without expectation or judgment. You are aware of your body in this moment in time, paying attention to everything that is now. You are present just in this moment, observing all in a non- judgmental way. You place all your attention, to the extent you can control it, to this present moment and nothing else.

"Mindfulness" training is available online and many free programs are available for free viewing and practice on YouTube. "Mindfulness" practice is a way to calm and reprogram your brain to feel calmer and healthier. MRI studies in seniors who practiced "Mindfulness" for 30 minutes, 3 times a week have significant growth in grey matter in their brains, which suggests that there are a multitude of ways this practice will improve your mental state as well as your physical health.

In our current world, technology and multiple sources of stimulation bombard us almost constantly. People forget how to talk to one another, and the more disconnected we become, the more miserable and depressed we become. One recent study on depression linked it to the amount of time spent daily with technology. Over 2 hours daily of interaction with technology worsens depression. It's important to participate in activities that involve your spending time face to face with others, and it's important to feel needed and useful. A sense of purpose in life is important to feeling happy, as well as a feeling of connectedness to one's community. That requires an effort to participate in activities that foster connections to others.

So "Happiness," while elusive, is not as far out of our reach as you might think. About 40% of it is a result of conscious activities and choices you make in your day to day living. By making a choice to improve your quality of life and mental health with "Mindfulness" practice, your life can change.

The only thing you can control is yourself. The only behavior you can control is your own. Act in ways that display your goals and your truths. Keep your word to yourself and others will help you feel better about yourself. Make daily goals you can keep today. Allow time to rest and know that the more you like yourself and nurture yourself today, the healthier and happier your tomorrow will be.

Besides the YouTube Mindfulness resources, your phone applications can actually be useful here. "Insight Timer" and "Simple Habit" are two Apps that can help you practice Mindfulness easily and anywhere. Both of these offer thousands of Mindfulness options. All you need to do is pick one, get comfortable, close your eyes, and listen. Over time and with practice, Mindfulness changes your brain. Like any exercise, your ability to perform it improves and gets easier over time. Eventually you are able to calm yourself voluntarily whenever you need to. Using a combination of Mindfulness practice with positive and present thinking can be a powerful aide towards happiness, strong self -esteem, and self - confidence.

Here are a few examples of some Mindfulness activities:

Mindfulness Body Scan

Lay down comfortably. Mentally scan your body and pay attention to each body area and how it feels

If it feels tense see if you can imagine breathing calm into that body area and imagine your breath going there

If it feels uncomfortable see if you can imagine some healing energy going right to that spot. Continue to scan and practice these visualizations for calm and healing

Morning Mindfulness Practice

Sit comfortably. Perform a meditative breathing exercise such as counting to 4 to slow down each inhale and exhale

Set your intention for the day to do as many kind things as possible and visualize some ways you can be kinder to yourself and others around you

If your mind gets distracted by something upsetting, imagine a way that showing kindness to yourself helps you feel better

Don't forget to visualize things you have to do today that may be challenging. Imagine how you'll be patient, loving, and kind towards yourself and others as you do this challenging thing
Morning mindfulness practice

Mindfulness exercise: Three things
Recommended by Dr. Dawn Levitan-Counselor, Coach and Author of HELP Life Coaching Cards Toolkit and App

1. Sitting quietly, pay attention to the sounds you hear and identify three sounds.

2. Pay attention to your body, what are three things you feel.

3. Think of three things that made you happy or that you feel grateful for.

> *Pain is Inevitable. Suffering is optional.*
>
> *-Haruki Murakami, Author*

Even when bad things happen, we have to find a way to survive them. We have to find a way to forgive if only to let bad feelings go. We have to understand that this world is full of many hurt people who go on to hurt others. Some don't care. Some hurt intentionally and some hurt accidently. Either way, if we hang on to those hurts we give them the power to destroy our current lives. And if we hang on to too many we make ourselves very ill.

If we live our lives today, being grateful for whatever we have today, and being present in appreciating what we have today, we create our future happiness and our health, both mentally and physically. We can't change
what happened yesterday, but we have to do our best to create the live mindfully today doing the best we can, appreciating all we can and enjoying all we can, because truly, all we really have is now. Today and how you live it, creates your tomorrow.

Yoga As a Form of Mindfulness Practice

I have been practicing yoga now for about 14 years. I started doing it at age 50. I could barely move. I was shocked to realize how out of shape I was and how much mobility I had lost. I was still exercising regularly, so I had no idea of how much I couldn't do.

I would ride on the recumbent bike for an hour, and I thought that was pretty great, but I had no idea how stiff and immobile I had become. The stretching of yoga was very new, and I remember even the simplest positions and stretches being challenging and uncomfortable, which scared me to try them. But something happened each week as I practiced. The uncomfortable positions began to become less so, and my flexibility gradually returned.

My sense of discovery and accomplishment as I watched this occur was encouraging and I continued on. Over months I began to be able to do more challenging poses. Then I began to feel stronger and healthier than I've ever felt in my whole life, and happier too. At some point I began doing a little studying about the philosophical basis to yoga, and then I understood why.

Yoga is a health practice that originated in India, developed to enhance mental, physical and spiritual health. The goal of yoga is to learn to turn off the mental chatter, or monkey brain as it is referred to, that noise in our heads that makes us stressed and miserable. Yoga gradually trains you to pay attention to your breathing and teaches you to control it. It teaches you to breathe through stress. It trains you to quiet your busy brain. It makes you stronger and healthier. And it's the best pain management I've ever found. The inactive body becomes painful as muscles, ligaments and other connective tissue shrinks when unused. That causes pain. Yoga releases the tension and your body can move with less discomfort.

Then there are also the names of the yoga poses.

Names like "Warrior 1,2,3", these are empowering names. Just thinking of the name of the pose when you are in it, especially when you are feeling sad or vulnerable can change your perspective, especially the position of strength "Warrior 2." I don't think it's possible to be in this pose and not feel strong.

Yoga is also the best form of anti-aging available. You are actually learning to combine breath with movement, and at the same time, you're practicing "Mindfulness," all of which helps you feel and look younger. All that blood rushing to your head, when it's been stuck in your legs because we do too much sitting, has the power to strengthen and refresh.

There are many different types of yoga and these can be as different as apples and oranges. It's like calling what we speak a language, and then thinking all languages are alike. You have to try and expose yourself to many different types of yoga to find the one that speaks to your needs. The most important elements are breathing, attention to the moment, and the movement.

Yoga is exercise, and all exercise is hard. I often warn my patients that they are likely to hate it before they love it, and that can be part of the process. It's wonderful that people in the U.S. and elsewhere are getting more exposure to yoga at earlier ages to find out what it can do for you. But most importantly, I'd describe a good yoga class as a movement exercise you do to help your brain.

The most important point of doing yoga is for the quiet brain you achieve by the end of the class during "shivastana" or corpse pose. Yoga was designed as a practice to develop internal peace and happiness through meditation. One can't sit and meditate if one is distracted by thoughts or by pain, so the physical exercise was designed to prepare body and brain to sit quietly and peacefully for an extended period of time afterwards. Some people say they can't do it because it's "too slow" for them, but that's exactly what they need. They need to cultivate that internal silence. There are reasons a good yoga class involves a live teacher, so you have options to modify the practice if there's something you can't do. There are reasons you need to leave the home, and leave your phone and purse and wallet and shoes outside of the room. You need to hear someone else's voice outside your head. You need to leave worldly distractions behind to fully benefit. The more years you spend doing yoga, the more clearly you begin to understand that yoga is always a practice, and each practice is an opportunity to experience or learn something new. The focus is the process, not the outcome. When you begin to think of the class something you're practicing instead of something you need to achieve, your whole perspective changes.

There are many different types of yoga and it's important to go to a studio where you feel comfortable. Familiarize yourself with some of the terms before you go, to increase your comfort. Let the instructor know that you are new to yoga. You're going to be barefoot, and common courtesy is that you aren't super dirty or stinky. You're sharing space and time with other people, and want to be respectful. There are many different types of yoga and some can be quite intimidating. Bikram for example, is practiced in a 105 degree room. This is not a practice for beginners. Nor is Ashtanga yoga. Both of those practices do the same routine at every class. This could appeal to you and if so, see if you can find a class for beginners. Bikram has students situated according to expertise, with the best students in the front of the class. This is very different from most practices which involve what's called Vinyasa yoga, or a practice that varies each time and links breath with movement. Find out as much as you can about a studio and the style of yoga practiced there before you go. Ask if you can watch a class. Watch the people who are leaving the class; if they look relaxed and happy, you've probably found a good location to check out. When I leave a good class, I feel like I've had an hour of massage and an hour of supportive psychotherapy! At the end of class, it's common for members to adopt what looks like a prayer position and say "Namaste." This is not a prayer at all, but is a recognition of the light of spirit that resides in each one of us, in our personal journey. The translation of "namaste" means "the light in me recognizes the light in you," essentially wishing others to find peace in their life journey.

Yoga begins with physical practice but actually has 7 branches of study to prepare for the 8th stage of "bliss". Yama is the first branch and deals with how we conduct ourselves and our integrity. Yama encourages nonviolence, truthfulness, honesty, continence of character and avoiding jealousy. Niyama is the second limb and deals with self discipline and spiritual practices. These include cleanliness, contentment, passion, study of one's self and sacred scriptures, and surrender to a higher power. The postures practiced in yoga are the Asanas, the third limb, which is about knowing your body better and developing your spirituality. Pranayama is the fourth limb, which focuses on cultivating and controlling the breath.

Pratyahara refers to the fifth limb, involving withdrawal from the physical world to focus on the internal. Dharana is the sixth limb which focuses on developing the mental concentration to control your thoughts and focus on one thing, preparing you for the seventh limb, meditation, or Dhyana. This involves being keenly aware without focus in a state of a quieted mind. These practices lead to the 8th stage, a state of bliss or ecstasy.

I'd like to share a personal story about the power and benefits of yoga. My mother was turning 85, and I happened to be extremely angry with both my parents as this hallmark date approached (because of something hurtful they did to someone close to me). My mother was used to a yearly family trip to Las Vegas but in my anger I had no desire to go. People don't turn 85 every day and I felt obligated. My sister would be on another flight, and with my father's immobility and dementia, and mom's limited mobility, this would
involve traveling with two disabled people, not something I was looking forward to. As expected, there were a number of moments that were incredibly sad and difficult. But I had yoga to turn to.

I went to a yoga class before I got my parents on that plane. And I'm glad I did because traveling with them that day, feeling as angry as I was, (did I mention I hate flying anyway?) was one of the hardest days of my life. But I got through it, and then I went to a yoga class the next day, and it was worth the $70 I paid in cab fare to get there and back. The class I found was perfect, it almost made me cry how incredibly healing it was.

Everyone there was so warm and friendly, and the teacher was fantastic and talked a lot about healing. I went again the following day, and I felt energized and happy again. Coming home was much, much easier. I went to yoga the next morning after I returned. Yoga was a wise gift I gave myself. I realized that the reason yoga is so powerful is that it brings you back to yourself. Yoga brings you back to the you that is without the stress, without all the noise, and is one of the most wonderful gifts you can give yourself.

Strengthen Your Forgiveness Skills

Forgiveness is another great skill to develop. Making a commitment to a process that involves letting go of hurt you have carried with you for years is another gift you give yourself. The time frame is ongoing and the result is feeling lighter and happier. Like everything else you might have as a personal goal it takes practice, time and patience but pays off long term. Like the difference with a crash diet vs changing your life style in eating more healthy daily in some way, the differences it makes are gradual but add up over time, and the result is greater happiness. Forgiveness involves compassion and love for yourself.

Dr. Fred Luskin has written a number of books to help foster forgiveness skills, most well know is his "Forgive For Good." Forgiveness is about taking back the power to decide how you feel about what happens to you. It is a trainable skill that gets better with practice. It takes you out of the victim role and helps you to a place of health and healing".

While many of the people who have hurt us don't "deserve" forgiveness, this is clearly about relinquishing the anger and negativity to unload it from the burden you are carrying. The reason one small scowl or negative word or behavior can "ruin your whole day" is that it triggers some hurt you've been carrying around for a long time. The longer it takes to get over daily hurts, the bigger and longer you've been carrying that baggage. The solution is to watch your reactions, understand the triggers and choose to let it go. How?

Let's just consider how we got here. 50% of us were lucky enough to grow up in a loving, healthy, emotionally nourishing family. The rest of us, not so much. That means there are an awful lot of us broken souls walking around who are wounded. If you didn't learn that love and trust were your birthrights, then you have a lot of work to do to feel happiness in your life. That begins when you take responsibility for it and work to do everything you can every day to be loving and compassionate to yourself. Do you believe every child deserves love? What could you have possibly done as a baby or small child to have been so punished, or neglected? The answer is nothing. All babies and children are lovable. What happened to you is unfair.

But carrying that around with you all your life only destroys you.

How could you change that perspective? Perhaps by using Visualization Techniques, things you can imagine that are healing. You might begin with thinking about some childhood experiences as they pop up in your mind, but this time imagine a different scenario. Createthe scenario with a loving parent, sibling or friend and how it would have felt so different. The new scenario you are imagining is yourself loving your small self the way you deserved to be loved and treated. Powerful stuff there, and healing, because with this scenario you begin to say to yourself and imagine yourself healing you, and more amazing that it works. When you practice doing this enough, loving and healing your small self and soothing yourself, you have come far in learning an important skill towards self-calming. You know how to fix it and have the power to fix it. When you have learned this, you have developed the power to create your own daily happiness.

When someone does something in the present that triggers a really strong response that crushes you, you can snap back to when you were victimized before. If that happens, the first step is always to calm down. You have to calm down enough to be able to figure outwhat's going on and how you're going to get over it. Look around you. You are not in that situation now. Be compassionate and patient with yourself. Breathe. Do a breathing exercise. You can handle it.

Sometimes when you feeling powerless, you just become and stay angry. Anger keeps you in a place of pain, but if feels much better. Anger is protective in that way, we go from feeling victimized and weak to angry and powerful- but that anger not only protects you right now, it continues to keep others from getting close to you and pushes them away. That's not a healthy way to live.

147

How do you get to forgiveness?

Here are some helpful steps taken from Dr. Luskin's research and writings.

> 1. Forgive yourself first. The mistakes you've made were never your intention, were they? You were doing your best.
>
> 2. Assume the same thing about the person who hurt you. Assume they were also doing their best or try to imagine what hurts they might have experienced in their lives to make them act how they did.
>
> 3. Do your best to find some positive out of the experience. Maybe it made you stronger, or you learned something new about yourself and how tough you are, that despite what has happened you've been able to pick up the pieces of your life and move on. Many of the parents from the Sandy Hook shootings have become very actively involved in gun control and mental health efforts. The worst events still provide us an opportunity to do something positive in the name of what we've lost. Observe and read about others who have overcome adversity; because you might find a link to what helped them put that in their past. Sometimes thinking about what others have survived can help us realize our situation in comparison isn't insurmountable and we can be grateful our trial is not as horrible as theirs, and that can give us something to be grateful for.

148

*(Read "Unbroken" by Laura Hillibr or "A
Mother's Reckoning; Living in the
Aftermath of Tragedy" by SueKlebold)*

*4. Be kind, very kind to yourself, and slow
down your breathing. The reason
practicing Yoga can be so healing is that it
teaches us to breathe, and that we can
breathe, even while trying to do something
that is very difficult or impossible. The
knowledge that we can master and recover
from this situation as long as we keep
breathing will give you courage to face
what you fear.*

*5. Practice Mindfulness. This is another
way you gradually re-wire your brain to
slow down and feel better*

Forgiveness exercise

How do you get from the point where you've
exaggerated the grievance to a point of obsession?
First write down everything you can remember about
the offense and why it's been so harmful and painful
for you. This is your "grievance story". The more
you carry around this story, the stronger it becomes. It
keeps the injury fresh and keeps you locked in the
past.

Now write the apology letter you wish you would
have received. Incorporate all the elements of an
effective apology: include an expression of remorse,
acknowledgement of the offense, an explanation of the
behavior, an attempt to fix or remedy the situation,

and reassurance that the person is doing something to prevent this from occurring again. Write this from the perspective of the hurtful person.

Mail this to yourself. As you put it in the mailbox, use the affirmation "I am letting this go".

Now write your survival story. Write optimistically about your life 5 years from now. Write about how you survived and overcame that hardship. Write about what you learned about yourself and how you learned to get stronger. Accept the apology that you wrote. If you need to forgive yourself, pretend to be the other person accepting your apology and imagine receiving the forgiveness.

Think of times you have been granted forgiveness. Notice when someone is kind to you after you have hurt them.

Notice how often you naturally forgive those you like or love.

Every day that you do something different from yesterday is a success. Work towards forgiving yourself and those around you for all our human imperfections. You'll be healthier and happier if you do.

Notice when someone is kind to you after you have hurt them.

Notice how often you naturally forgive those you like or love.

Every day that you do something different from

yesterday is a success. Work towards forgiving yourself and those around you for all our human imperfections. You'll be healthier and happier if you do.

Building Self Esteem

"I've learned that people will forget what you said, people will forget what you did, but people will never forget how you made them feel." Maya Angelou said it perfectly. We are all navigating this life with our own baggage, our own stuff.

I heard it said the other day that if we keep looking backwards, we can't see where we're going, but much of the time that's exactly where we live, in our own minds, either focused ahead or behind us. We can miss the gift of life right in front of us if we do. We can imprison ourselves in our own heads, and forget that each time we venture out, there is likely an opportunity to engage with others. There are also small things we can do every day to shore up our self esteem and like ourselves more. My suggestion here is to pick one of the following areas and just practice that goal for a week before moving on to another.

Here are a few things you can do to change your perspective.

Start the day focusing on the positive.

1. Today, identify one thing you like about yourself. Maybe it's your feet, maybe it's your hair, your nails, your skin. It doesn't matter what anyone else thinks but it does

matter that you find something you like about yourself and acknowledge it. Can you think about this characteristic and let yourself feel proud of it? Try.

2. Can you make a list of some of your good qualities? Just acknowledge them first. Take a deep breath and let that sink in a moment. Now, can you use that positive quality to do something nice for someone else today? Even a stranger? Or even for someone you're not particularly fond of? You're a great baker? Make something for a neighbor. Bring something into the office. Pay attention to and acknowledge the positive comments you receive.

3. Quiet the chatter. The worst thing we do to make ourselves miserable is to obsess about something that upsets us. How do you quiet your brain? Do something brand new that you've never done before. It requires your full attention. Do something difficult. It improves your self esteem because you dared to try it. Do something you're afraid of. The mastery of your fear increases your confidence. Do something silly, laughter is a great healer. Start a conversation with a stranger, who knows what you will learn. Strive to learn something, open your mind to do so. Shonda Rhimes, the successful producer,

decided to make herself the year of "Yes",
as result of saying yes , she lost over 100
pounds and wrote a book about it. You
never know where new avenues can lead
you. Dare to be brave.

Set realistic goals and be a person of your word

Your words define you, and the conversations you
have with yourself are important. It's important to
speak to yourself in the present moment. Our brains
don't understand negatives very well, so if you have a
goal to not eat cake or not overeat, that's a goal the
brain doesn't recognize. It understands the concrete
information "cake" and "eat." So the exact opposite
of what you wanted occurs, you tell yourself not to eat
the cake and you eat the cake. How you talk to
yourself and how it's phrased is very important. If
instead of "I won't eat cake" you take the time to
imagine yourself looking at the cake, admiring it, but
deciding to skip it because you want to fit into those
pants, you've programmed a new positive message.
You practice doing this in your thoughts enough and it
will be much easier to actually perform that action
when the cake presents itself.

Goals have to be presented to ourselves in the
positive and in the future. So a very big part of our
self- esteem issues is based on our self-talk. It is
important to be a person who keeps their word,
especially to yourself. If every day you tell yourself
you are going to do something and don't, it becomes a
day you destroy your self-esteem. Every time you tell
yourself "I'll do that tomorrow" is a day you have
created disappointment in yourself which leads to low

self- esteem and depression.

When you set a goal, it's imperative that you set one that is truly attainable today. It has to be within your grasp, and within your ability to accomplish it today. Each today creates your tomorrow. So instead of focusing on the 10-20-30 lbs you want to lose, your goal today might be to set a meal plan for today that you can follow today. Changing yourself involves doing one thing different. Every change we make today creates something new. I have often asked patients who want to lose weight to just do one thing different from what they did the day before. One small step towards that ultimate goal, that can be accomplished today. That's the way you build self-esteem. You set yourself a goal for today that you know you can keep and you do it. When you accomplish one small thing, it improves your mood and how you feel about yourself, and leads to the next small step. Eventually trial and error will help you figure out the changes you can successfully make and live with today. Those are the changes that last. It's also the reason why diets don't work, because deprivation and misery don't result in success. Success leads to more success. Maybe the one small step you could make would be to start logging your intake, start writing down everything you eat. Doing this makes you much more aware of what you consume. Most of us consume without any thought or awareness and don't even realize what we're doing much of the time. Just writing down what you actually put in your mouth will increase your consciousness of your behavior, and that awareness will begin a change in your behavior with food. So that is the first goal. Maybe a second step could be figuring out if there is one day in the coming week where you could commit to limiting

your caloric intake to the suggested amount. Or eat without distraction- no TV, phone etc.
Eat Mindfully. Pay attention to how each bite tastes and how it makes you feel. Pause after each bite.

Is your goal to "get in shape"? You're already ashape! That's too ill defined and you can't measure it, so break it down. If you're not exercising at all, is there one small thing you can do right now? Like right now, could you walk in place for 5 minutes while you're reading the rest of this paragraph. Voila – you exercised today. You are much more likely to achieve success when you make your goals as specific, and as small and attainable as possible. We change gradually just by being more aware. Listen to your internal voice. Correct it when you're phrasing goals too vaguely and make them more specific. Doing one thing today towards your long-term goal is improves your ability to feel good about yourself, and becoming a person who keeps their word to themselves is the way to become that person.

Find Your Purpose

In the early 1940s, the rate of infant mortality was very high. Abroad it was even higher. In 1944 a study was done in the United States to determine the effectiveness of touch vs just nutrition. Forty babies were divided in two groups. Those who got all their physical needs met but no affection and those who were cared for by caregivers who were allowed to play and speak to the babies. The study was stopped after 4 months, because half of the babies in the basic needs group had died.

In 1952, Dr Rene Spitz studied a group of infants raised in an orphanage/hospital environment versus those raised by women prisoners in their cells. The institutional group had a 37% death rate, but none of the babies raised in prisons died.

These and other studies documented the need of human affection and touch and greatly changed the behaviors and rules for childbirth and visitation in our country over the years. In the 1950s, moms were sent home when children had medical issues and were allowed only limited contact with children in intensive care or after birth. Things like fathers and partners allowed in the birth rooms and less visiting restrictions after birth today have changed because human contact and love goes a long way to promote life and survival. Dr. Leo Buscalglia made the promotion of the need for touch his professional crusade in the 1970s. Long before Oprah and Dr Phil, Leo gave broadcasts preaching his gospel encouraging the hug. He used to say that hugs were necessary to health, and he encouraged people to give and take as many as possible daily. He made hugging his life's purpose.

Anything can be your purpose. Perhaps being the best daughter or son or father or mother is your purpose. In building self-esteem, there's nothing as powerful as what occurs when we connect do things for someone else, and make that our purpose. We all need to feel connected to others. We all need to feel that we matter. But often, what impacts us the most are the things we do, and that others do for us that require only effort and time.

I help coordinate an "Empty Bowls Event" which is a fundraiser where potters and other artists donate their work, but the focus is on soup type bowls. Our version is one inspired by the Michigan high school students who started the event in about 1969. The bowls are sold and with each bowl purchase a simple soup kitchen type meal of soup and bread is served to remind us lucky ones that there are others whose only meal is what they get that day from a soup kitchen or pantry. The money raised is donated to food pantries and soup kitchens in the surrounding area. One year a woman came in to the event with three children and bought just one bowl. That would only entitle them to one bowl of soup. I offered this woman an extra three soup tickets so all the children could eat. She refused this, and explained to me that her family was one of the "customers" of the food pantry, and she wanted to teach her children that no matter how poor one is, there is always a way to help others. A powerful lesson for her children, and incredibly moving, she gave me a gift that day! Extending kindnesses to others no matter how dire our situation continues to be a path to internal wealth and happiness. When we are encountering the people in Santa hats ringing their Christmas Bells by the Salvation Army Pot, it's so easy to see who is doing it because they "have to" and others who are full of happiness and joy! The ones singing and really trying to spread the joy of the season are people who themselves are joyful. They may be joyful to have a job, joyful to give back to the organization that helped them off the streets or gave them a roof over their head, or joyful in their sobriety. We forget and take so much for granted every day and focus far too much on what is missing from our lives. An attitude adjustment and a change in our moods can be obtained so easily from taking our focus off what we don't have and looking outwards.

I remember in my early years of working in Psychiatric Nursing, people always asked me if working with depressed people wasn't depressing to me. On the contrary, the more depressed I was or upset about something in my personal life, going to work put it all in perspective for me. As sad as I was, I was still able to function, and like the lady buying the soup bowl, I was grateful because I still had something to give, I could still function in spite of how miserable I felt, and the people who received my efforts were appreciative.

Feeling useful helps us feel better about ourselves.

Even thinking about how you can do something for someone else can begin to put a smile on your face and change your perspective. Paying the road toll for the person behind you, buying the coffee for the person behind you, handing a free coupon to someone for an item you have extra coupons for…..there are millions of ways we can do something for someone else which will brighten your day and theirs. Even in the course of working, a kind word about how well someone is doing their job can provide a nice lift for someone else.

Being connected to others and feeling useful in our daily lives, even when it's because we've done something small for someone else, can go a long way in improving our happiness and our self-esteem. There are so many ways we can contribute to the world. No matter how little we have to offer, just our time can be of great service to others. Volunteer work is a wonderful opportunity to see a bit of the world you wouldn't see otherwise. There is nothing quite as wonderful as how you feel when you contribute something to someone else. There is no one that doesn't have the ability to do something for someone else. Push yourself out to do one thing for someone else.

Pick an organization or cause you care about and volunteer. Work is work, you're expected to go there and do your job. Home is home; you have an expected place and role there. Volunteering puts you in a whole new life circle. There are new people you will meet, new things you will see. There are also new things you will learn. I read about an 84 year old woman who lived near an army base. She went to her nearby airport every day and welcomed back the soldiers who returned with a hug for many years. She was known as Fort Hood's "hug lady" and recently died. What a beautiful
legacy.   There are many ways we can all help the world be a better place. No one else needs to know but you to feel better about yourself.

Your purpose could be to validate someone else's hard work and accomplishments. Sometimes it's extremely helpful to just have someone present who knows where you came from and what you achieved. It is a powerful gift to acknowledge their hard work. Sometimes just validating what someone else has accomplished or what they are going through or what they are feeling is exactly what they need.

If you break out what I believe most of our purpose is, the most basic is to love and be loved, and to be part of a community. If you provide this to just one person, even just to yourself, you have done a lot, because if you provide this to yourself, your heart is full of love and that helps you to share this with others. Your purpose might be just to heal yourself.

Your purpose might be to raise and launch healthy children. Your purpose might be to leave your neighborhood a little cleaner after the dog walk then before you went on it. There are many ways we can find to be more connected to our purpose, which intensifies and improves the quality of our life and those who pass through it. Give a little thought today to your purpose and watch how you feel and people around you respond to your efforts.

Try looking at things from a different perspective

You know that old saying about seeing the world with rose colored glasses on? Of course it refers to people who are only seeing what they want to see, and missing the negatives. But people who are feeling lonely, depressed, or negative all the time are definitely wearing a different pair of glasses. Let's call those the "Victim" glasses. They go through their lives taking every negative thing personally. The person who cuts them off in traffic or doesn't allow them to merge is one more jerk out to destroy them or make them miserable.

Depression and anger does that to you. It makes you feel like a victim. Anger makes you feel out of control.

I had a beautiful young woman in my office recently. One of many I have seen with eating disorders. She sees herself as fat no matter how thin she is, she dwells every day in the misery of her hunger and weakness, because she sees food as her enemy and eating it as a weakness and lives in such fear of obesity that she could die of starvation. This is an extreme case of course, but is a perfect example of how the "glasses" we wear every day distort our perceptions of what is real, in front of us, available and good. How is this pair of glasses different than the one who sees everyone as out to hurt them and walks around in constant pain? Very few of us actually achieve the body perfection we see on TV and magazines. But if you take off those glasses skewing your vision, you can actually look for different images that will blow your mind if you notice them! You can actually find dozens of imperfect people around you every day that actually seem happy I try to explain to people all the time that you don't have to look attractive to everyone, you just need to find one person who is able to see the beauty in your soul! And to do that, you need to let the beauty shine! You don't have to look beautiful to be beautiful. You have to feel good about yourself and feel you have something to offer others. And by the way, look at the people who are perpetually alone? They are looking for fantasy perfection, and will reject the imperfect in favor of being alone. I feel very sorry for them. Once I did a presentation to a group of singles for a dating organization, and a 68 year old woman was talking to me afterwards about a man she had met on a park bench earlier that day. She had ended up talking to him for 3 hours, but said she would never think of dating such a person because of one physical attribute he had. I had to laugh to myself, here she said she was tired of being alone, and had just met someone whose company she enjoyed for 3 hours, and then rejected him. Love is about friendship and companionship. Attraction is lovely but with time the majority of the time spent in relationships is about emotional intimacy, not physical intimacy.

So what glasses are you wearing? Are you

constantly walking around wearing "ugly" "unlovable" "victim" or "angry" glasses? The glasses you are looking at the world with define your feelings about yourself and your ability to connect with others. If you're feeling badly about yourself, you avoid eye contact, you avoid conversations, and you avoid a million ways to connect with others who are good people. Not every one of us will be lucky to find that "perfect" partner, and partly that is because we have to have faith in ourselves and others in order to do so. We have to be able to take the leap to trust that actually the vast majority of people in the world are good, and their being nice to you doesn't always mean they want something from you. Who do you love? Are those people perfect? Is perfection attainable? Seeking perfection is another way to doom yourself to failure. It is impossible! Look up and around you. Watch the people who seem happy. Yes, they have found a way to navigate the world in spite of all the tremendous fears it holds. They have a found a way to be okay in spite of all their imperfections. And they have found ways to love others in spite of their imperfections. They have found acceptance. Perhaps you could just take off those glasses for a little while, long enough to look around you. Go somewhere where there are lots of people and watch them. Happy successful people get that way because at some point they believed in themselves enough to get out there and find what made them happy.

Be good at one thing

I remember hating myself when I was younger, hating how I looked and felt and hating my life. When you're struggling you tend to over-focus on all the things that are wrong. You're hurting, and your pain skews how you see yourself and your life. From the Cognitive Behavioral standpoint, there is an error in your thinking. When you're doing this, you're generalizing to believe the current bad thing going on will never end. Nothing will ever go right, and you will never like yourself. When you think in this distorted way, everything feels too overwhelming and it's hard to know where to start even when you know you need to change.

One way is to pick one thing at which you excel. Every person is or can be good at something. I have this completely useless skill where I have amazing voice recognition. I can hear an actors' voice and relate it to all the other movies or television shows where I have seen (or heard) that same actor. Watching the new animated movies or listening to narrations on commercials is fun for me because I can often figure out who are the actors behind the voices. This "skill" has absolutely no value in life whatsoever, unless you can include annoying people as a "skill" because no one else really cares, but my husband will humor me looking things up on Google to show him that I was right. It's silly, but it makes us laugh. I can choose what I want to do with this silly skill, so I use it to amuse myself. Every skill doesn't really need to have a purpose. It just has to be something that makes you smile about you. When you were a child, do you remember how funny it was for someone to burp out the alphabet? It's hilarious! Having things about you that are funny is wonderful. Laughter is wonderful. Making people laugh is wonderful. What a gift!

You literally can pick any little thing and work at it to excel. You can work on being a better greeter of people (sometimes I visualize I'm a dog when people come over, I imagine my tail wagging as I go up to greet them, because otherwise I'm a terrible greeter). You can work at cleaning off your desk every night before you leave. You can work at having the cleanest floor you've ever had before. You can write the best thank you notes anyone has ever seen. You can become the best chocolate chip cookie maker anyone knows. My cousin is the best at picking the most beautiful and thoughtful birthday cards to send. My sister-in- law is the best person I have ever known when it comes to sending things to people's children. One of my nephews is the kindest person I have ever known- he hugs everyone. Each of us has a unique special skill. And if you think you have none, you just haven't uncovered your unique skill.

Every failure is an opportunity to learn to do something different. The decisions you make each day about what you do and how you do them are opportunities to change and improve yourself. Learning something new every day is another way. Every discomfort is an opportunity to explore, an opportunity to figure out if there's some way you can approach it differently. Learn a card trick. Memorize a favorite famous speech. Read a joke and share it with someone else. There are many things you can get better at, both large and small, and ones that cause smiles in you and others are great places to start. Pick any little challenge and get better at it, then pick another, and another. Laugh at yourself, it's ok to fail. It's ok not to be the best. It's ok to be you.

Embrace the pain life brings you

We are programmed to think of pain as being a bad thing, but pain has many functions for us. It warns us away from things that are bad. It tells us when to reach out to others and get help. It is easier to think about how to deal with physical pain than it is to deal with psychological pain. When we have physical pain, it's easier to think of something to "do" to "fix" it, but when you experience chronic pain either physically or psychologically, it becomes much more challenging to "fix."

Discussing physical pain first, it's very interesting to read studies on Mindfulness and pain. Two different people can experience the same degree of pain, and one person may find it overwhelming and another as a mild annoyance. How we react is very personal, but research does show us that how we think about pain and what we do about it can impact the degree of effect it has on our lives. People who practice "Mindfulness" actually experience pain as less severe and recover quicker.

People who are instead focused on relieving all pain and numbing themselves to it, don't function well at all

Because pain is a part of life.

Sometimes it is a matter of the way we let ourselves think of what is happening to us. When we think of a situation as painful, we do actually feel more pain versus thinking of a situation as challenging. Case in point again is Matthew Sanford who I discussed in Yoga. He wrote a book called "Waking." Matthew is inspirational without a doubt, but it is also how he took what happened to him and incorporated that disability into a part of his life that enhanced his life, rather than destroyed it. His paralysis was a challenge, not an obstacle. He found new ways to do things. Sometimes tragedies can also lead to opportunities. Healthy people find ways to cope. How well you do this affects your life quality.

When something bad happens, what thought processes do you have? Does the situation seem insurmountable? Do you go to a place of feeling like a loser, or a failure? "Bad" things happen regularly. Do you have a tendency to focus on what goes wrong instead of the thousands of things that go right every day? When things go wrong, whether it's emotional or physical, we tend to panic. If instead we consider these things in a different way, we might feel differently about them. I invite you to think of discomfort as a way the body has to tell you something needs to change in your life, and other feelings we think of as negative as an alarm telling you something. The alarm is telling you it's time to think about what you're doing, maybe it's telling you to think before you do things, or even stop what you're doing, but try not fighting or numbing these feelings, because if you do you're missing an opportunity to listen to what your body and brain are telling you- something needs to change.

What if instead of labeling it as "pain" you thought of it as an interesting sensation. Listen, explore, and figure out what it's trying to tell you. The solution to happiness is inside you, and you can only get there if you truly embrace what your body and brain is trying to tell you. Sometimes, you just have to stop and feel it. Let yourself cry. Let yourself grieve. Stop telling yourself you can't handle it because you can and will. Surround yourself as much as possible with those who love themselves and you. Only when you can tolerate pain and discomfort can you truly feel peace, happiness and gratitude because its absent. If you

spend all your time trying to avoid feeling bad, you
will always feel bad because running away doesn't
feel good and things have a way of popping back up
over and over again. The alternative is to keep
repeating the same life mistakes. So try embracing the
pain you feel, welcome the message it is giving you.
Spend less time fighting it, or trying to numb it, and
try to listen to the message.

When you're able to do that, you'll be able to
endure it and possibly find new ways to survive it.
Then you will be able to enjoy all the times it's absent.
You have to find a way to endure pain, because there
is no life without it.

Release pain when it's time to release it

We talked about embracing pain, but maybe you're
a person who's embracing it all the time. Just as
dangerous if not worse, is holding onto pain. Here's
why; when you hold onto pain the only one it is
hurting is you.

Listen to any victim's statements during a
sentencing hearing in any courtroom, and it is easy to
see who has held onto their pain and who has released
it. It's almost astounding, but at that statement or
perhaps in a communication later, the victims forgive
their perpetrators. Why is that? It is because
forgiveness is letting go and forgiveness is how you
heal.

There is no adult human alive with feelings who
hasn't been hurt, failed, rejected, or disappointed in

some way. Because of the job I do in mental health, I have heard more than my share of stories about how cruel humans can be to one another. Yet I know not one of those patients came to me to help them hold onto their pain, they came to me to help them release it. Releasing it is what this work of life is about. We don't ask for this pain, we ask for love. But loving involves hurt too. In order to feel your best, you have to know how to release it.

I'm a big fan of Mary Lambert's "Body Love" when she says "Fathers and uncles are not claiming your knife anymore, are not your razor, no, put the sharpness back. You are worth more… than a man's whim or your father's mistake. You are no less valuable as a size 16 than a size 4. You are no less valuable as a 32A than a 36C."

How many of us think our definition and value are about something others see? Yet just as many "beautiful" people are victims of the same pain, and sometimes even more so, and people in pain don't feel beautiful.

Physical pain is one thing, but if you focus too much on it, your whole life is about pain. The same is true of emotional pain. Bad things happen, but we have to learn how to forgive. How? I can only explain how I do it. But this is based on years of research, knowledge, and practice.

I've gotten pretty good at letting things go. I've had a lot of practice. I focus on what I can control and what good I can find in every situation. So there are people in my life, who like me, are not perfect. I try to rejoice in the love I get rather than obsess about the love I don't. I try to enjoy every project that turns out right, and I try to let go of what I fail at. I accept that I and others are only human and we all make mistakes. Sometimes I don't feel happy, but I can look at others' happiness and appreciate watching it like one might watch a beautiful painting or flower. I try to pay attention to all the beauty around me, and every little thing that's going right. When I'm really miserable, I get excited about running water, flush toilets, and that zombies aren't currently running around my streets. In other words, I try to pay attention to as much as I can to what's right and good in my life. I try to look at the pain, whether it's physical or emotional, as a sensation, something interesting, and then I try to pay attention to something else instead. Maybe I'm grateful for the new leaf growing out of a plant that maybe will be a flower someday. So this is what "Mindfulness" is. The more I pay attention to what is right and good in the present moment is how I stay calm and happy. It works for me and I hope you will try it.

Work on your likability

When I was growing up I was taught that if you want to be good at something, work hard. If you did your best and worked your hardest, you could learn anything and become a success. I did those things, and found out that this advice was actually wrong. It worked many years until I realized that it's more important to be likable than to do a good job! Shocking! I thought it would be enough to just work hard and be good at what I did! Not true! When opportunities for promotion arise, it's the relationships with your co-workers that probably end up counting more than your performance! The likeable boss has employees who work much harder for them. The

169

likeable boss validates your feelings and concerns and convinces you why it's in your best interest to do things their way. It wasn't until I realized I had to spend almost at least as much time cultivating work relationships as doing my job that I found true job success. And I was somewhat resentful of this at first too! Spending time socializing with my co-workers wasted time I could be working or having fun elsewhere, but not spending that time caused me frustration when it was time to promote a new idea or a change in policy or procedure. Because if people don't like you, they won't listen to what you say. When people like you, they root for you and they root for your success too. Liking you makes them happy to help you. Donald Trump is the best example. People have decided they like him on TV, so it doesn't matter to them how poorly he behaves. They like him so they support him. They want him to succeed. When people don't like you, they get pleasure in watching you fail or struggle, and that will only interfere with you achieving your goals.

When I lectured in class, I read the evaluations, took the criticisms to heart, and worked harder and harder to prepare better presentations. Then I watched other people do presentations. I noticed something similar in that setting as well. It was more important to engage the audience and make them like you and enjoy the presentation rather than be the expert presenting all the recent research and information. It actually worked better if less were taught! All the effort I was making to ensure I had the best and most accurate and detailed up to the minute medical information was not actually what people responded to. They didn't want to be impressed by my knowledge. They wanted to learn something but receive that information in a way that was interesting and entertaining. I got better responses focusing on engaging them with stories or photos, and by picking a few important points for them to learn.

I told this to one of my younger patients recently, and he was shocked. He also had focused too much on mastery of his craft and not enough in his relationships with his bosses, so had many problematic issues in his jobs. He also needed to work less and consider those social graces to be just as important in order for him to be successful in his work. If this is something that is a challenge to you, then spend as much time working on your social skills and collegial relationships as you have mastering the other skills and knowledge you
have. Because this may be even more important to your life success.

Chapter 5: Suicide Survival ; Recovery, Forgiveness, and Shame

This chapter is for those of you who are struggling with losing someone you cared about to suicide. It is meant to offer you some support. If you have just picked up this book, and turned to this chapter first, please go back to the Coping section after you're done reading this, as that section has specific techniques to use in the course of your healing.

It is also common, during the course of your healing, to contemplate suicide yourself. The pain of the loss mixed with the guilt of thinking you failed someone you care about is overwhelming. Whether you have actually failed them or not, it is common to feel as though you have. There can be a lot of shame in survival. Whenever we lose someone close, we think of all the times we could have done more to help them, but this is much worse in the case of a suicide. When we look back at the course of their behavior, sometimes it's easier to see in retrospect that there were some clues, like giving things away or saying goodbye in a different way than usual. The person who takes their own life leaves a skeleton of pain and shame for everyone who has ever passed their way.

All of us can always do better jobs of caring for our fellow humans, and all of us get wrapped up in our own personal demons and issues. We never know when is the last day we could see someone we love, whether we lose them by car accident or heart attack, but when those things happen to someone we love, who chooses to die, we grieve in a different way. When someone dies by suicide, we also blame ourselves. Suicide is a double edged sword.

We convince ourselves somehow that it's because we didn't do enough to save them. I know that for every patient I lose to suicide, I go through every action I've done to consider what I have missed or might have said that wasn't what they needed. There is an immediate sense of guilt that all close to the patient feel, which complicates and compounds the grieving process. This could be one of the factors that makes a survivor also more prone to contemplate suicide, because the combination of grief and guilt is overwhelming. It leaves a lifetime of shame with the message that we failed them.

Most suicide notes start with the words "I'm sorry", because the person doesn't really want to hurt you, they just don't see any other options for themselves. Everyone who knows the victim feels guilt. From the teacher to the neighbor, from the cousin to the bank teller, almost everyone who knows the person wonders if there is something they could have done differently. But this process is worst for those close to the person who died, who can continue to rehash what happened before the suicide and what they might have done differently. Even at the funeral or wake, the behavior of others is different and the community isn't sure what is acceptable to talk about and what isn't, so the support given the survivor is tempered with discomfort.

Such a complex mass of emotions makes it that the person who survives suicide takes much longer to reach any healthy state of recovery, and that person often carries a lifelong feeling of guilt. The survivor needs to recover from the loss and has to also forgive themselves, which can be even harder. It is not unusual for the person who has killed themselves, to have threatened it previously or even tried to suicide before. As a family member, you may or may not be aware of this. But when people find out someone has tried to kill themselves, after they recover from the fear and shock of this, they often convey anger that the person would do such a thing. During the period of anger, things can be said that are often of great regret.

One of my patients was having a fight with her live in boyfriend. During the fight things got heated, and when things are heated, people say a lot of things they don't mean. She did, and he said "I may as well just go kill myself" and in the heat of the moment, she replied, "yea, why don't you?" and he walked away and she just worked on calming herself down. And when she calmed down, she went to look for him. He was dead, hanging from a tree branch on their front lawn. What a horrible last conversation, and unfathomable guilt to recover from.

But this is not unusual. Many of my patients have said family members have said this to them, which makes them consider the act of suicide even more seriously. I'm sure these family members didn't really mean it, nor did the lady in the last paragraph mean it. In these situations, patients were needing to hear that their partner was angry but still important to them. Words are powerful. Sometimes we humans say some terrible things to each other. But it's never too late to apologize. We all are healthier as a community when we are kinder to each other, and being able to apologize for bad behavior is part of that kindness.

When a suicide occurs, as a community it's much more difficult to provide support if we don't know that's how a death occurs. Coroners will question family members and treatment providers after an accidental death. If there's no suicide note, and the stage is not so clearly that of a suicide, then the death is ruled accidental. A bottle of alcohol and an empty bottle of pills can be an accidental death. Single car accidents are often actually autocides. Coroners and police will do all they can to rule it accidental rather than call it a suicide, because it's so much easier to deal with an accidental death. Often those close to the person know it was likely a suicide or strongly suspect it, but never can discuss it. Suicide is against the law and is also a mortal sin in a number of religions. The family has to incorporate this shame as well and hide the truth, and this also keeps them from getting the support and help they actually need to recover.

In a completely different kind of scenario, a patient of mine recently came in and said that her work situation had improved greatly. Her boss, who was abusive to everyone at the office, had taken his life. What she found interesting was both how his second wife and stepdaughter looked so distraught, but also that she was able to talk to his adult son from his first marriage. The son was very confused by the large turnout from the company, as his father had always

175

been very emotionally abusive to him. She told his son the truth, that they were there because he was their boss and co-worker, because it was the right thing to do, that he was also abusive to them. That truth was actually very healing to the son, who was starting to feel he had been singled out for the abuse, and finding out that he was actually abusive to a lot of people was validating for him. If the son had never asked, and if my patient hadn't been honest, this very healing moment would have never happened.

In another situation, an older man I know planned to take his own life, but tried to do it while in the hospital so that his family wouldn't have to discover he had died. He stocked up on his sleeping pills and took them before he went into the hospital for a procedure. Needless to say, it wasn't a successful attempt. But he had written a suicide letter. It was close to 20 pages berating most of his family for failing him. I was able to intercede. After I read his letter, I discussed it with him. I was able to help him see the impact it would have had on them, and with his permission, I destroyed it. Instead he was given hospice care, which he hadn't realized was an option. He had a terminal condition, and I was able to explain to him that he wouldn't be in pain, and having a chance to say goodbye to his family was worthwhile. He had been an absentee father, his children were raised in foster care, but somehow in his mind, it was his children who hadn't been good enough to him in his life. The hospice setting made his death comfortable, but was also healing for him, his children, and his family.

The power of validation is one of the most healing tools we have in psychiatry, and among us humans to give to each other. Just hearing that things we are thinking and feeling are normal and acceptable, is a very powerful gift we can share. Sometimes the truth is the best gift we can give someone. Sometimes a white lie is. Being truthful with others, so they can provide us the support we need, so we feel less alone, can be the difference between living and dying. A typical grief support group will not help this family heal, they likely will need to work with a therapist. If they can find a support group for survivors of suicide, this would be the most helpful. In lieu of this, use your words to let the survivors know they are not alone, they are not to blame, and that they will likely need help to survive this healing process. Reading some of the Dr. Sidney Luskin books on Forgiveness would be very helpful, and a thoughtful gift for survivors.

Chapter 6: Case Studies and Discussion

If you are currently feeling depressed, or have recently thought of suicide, this may not be the time to read this chapter. Writing this chapter is what made me have to put this book aside for two years. Suicide is very depressing. It is very depressing about the wonderful people discussed here who took their lives. It is very depressing to realize that sometimes no matter what you do you can't always save everyone. The mind plays a trick on the people who feel overwhelmed and depressed and suicide is not always preventable. I suspect that as science progresses, we will identify a suicide genetic trait. There is already a trait identified associated with addiction, and one for sensitivity which can show which people are predisposed to developing PTSD. I have no doubt there will be a trait identified to explain why two people in the same circumstances respond very differently. One feels pain, but suicide would never cross their mind. The other feels the same pain and often has to fight with themselves not to act on suicidal thoughts, even when the trigger in retrospect seems small. Once these traits are identified, suicide will be less of a stigma, and hopefully more preventable. The mind, when it convinces itself something will never pass, can be very stubborn, unless science also finds a way to correct that trait.

I believe that Major Depression is a big factor in suicides, but Borderline Personality Disorder (BPD) may be a bigger factor. People with BPD experience incredibly painful moments without warning, that are overwhelming. The level of pain seems so intolerable, the brain convinced in that moment that nothing will ever get better, that the impulse to self- destruct seems insurmountable. There is not much pre- thought about suicide with BPD. It is done impulsively to cope. Those with Borderline Personality who cut themselves may have found a way to act on their thoughts in less severe fashion, but that becomes another source of shame. Those who understand they have Borderline Personality are hopefully in touch with experienced clinicians who can help them with their impulsive urges. Dialectical Behavior Therapy or DBT is a practice model that can be learned and should be pursued by those with this condition. People with BPD may suicide with little provocation. People with Depression provide some warning, and those in treatment are less likely to suicide. Both conditions are extremely painful states to live in, and both require much help and support.

It might be a fair statement to say that those who contemplate suicide are sensitive people who feel pain deeply. The world is a crowded and competitive place. We launch from parents and teachers who have told us everything we want to do is possible. Then we grow up and enter a world where we are constantly not good enough, smart enough, pretty enough, thin enough, talented enough.....and have to find a way to survive. In nature, we watch the mother eagle nudge the birds from the nest, because it's not until they begin to fall that they realize they can fly. But the falling is terrifying.

179

We watch the lives of the talented and successful in social media, and it seems like we can all be successful if we work hard. That is the myth of the American dream, isn't it?

For those who are artistic, and sensitive, competing for the few spots of those who want a certain high level of success in very competitive fields, can be a crushing experience. Even if we are the best at some talent, there is always someone who is better, or is trying to be better, or has better connections. We can be the star athlete in High School, or college, but then succeeding among the others who were also stars at their schools becomes harder and harder as the stakes get higher.

Each of the stories you're about to read are stories of either successful or interrupted suicides. As you read each story, there is something to be learned from each one, and there are points of discussion to ponder. I am hoping to finish this book before I have another story to add to this chapter, but working in this field one has to accept there are always lives teetering in the balance, and we're doing our best to help those who suffer. Recently, a colleague was hospitalized after one of his patients suicided. To think that these situations don't strongly affect the mental health of providers is naïve.

All of these stories are very sad, because these valuable humans left this world by their own hand. While you're reading these case studies you might ponder:

What did or might have changed the ending?

What might you have done different if you knew the person was in this much pain?

How did the events in their lives contribute to their choices? Was their action a well thought out plan or was it impulsive? Which risk factors contributed to the outcome? How would you feel if you knew this person?

What would you do if you were in this much pain? Would you tell anyone? Who would you tell? How do you think the different people in your life would respond?

What is your opinion on those who seek help for mental illness?

What is your opinion of those who take medications?

How would you feel if you had a mental condition that required you to take medication for years or possibly the rest of your life?

Are all suicides preventable? Is suicide ever justified? What is the role of religion in prevention of suicide?

Laura; suicide completed. Age 21.

Laura was a beautiful young woman who worked hard to become a professional dancer. She came from a loving family that included dedicated parents, and three brothers. But being successful in an industry like art, acting, music, or dance requires a thick skin

181

because it will always involve a lot of rejections and criticism. This vocational choice where being good at something won't guarantee success, can be a challenge. People who can be your cast mates and colleagues in one production will be competing with you for the next role; this doesn't create an atmosphere that fosters long term close relationships. Laura was committed to putting in the time and energy to be a success. She worked hard to handle her depression which came and went over the years. But in the year after one of her close supporters, her grandmother passed, the pain became too much to bear.

Laura never woke up one morning after taking a few too many pills, along with alcohol. She was 21.

There was no suicide letter left. Laura's death was an "accident" but Laura wrote her thoughts in her journals for many years, and her family knew it was suicide. She had been suicidal and depressed before. Her journals display the inner turmoil she felt about her feelings, and whether people liked her or not, and about whether she could be successful. She didn't feel she fit in, she didn't feel understood by others and she didn't understand others. She often wrote confused feelings about rejecting others and being rejected and hurt by them. Some of her journal entries can give us a picture into her tormented thoughts.

Here are some excerpts from some of her journals (courtesy of her family).

Journal entry, August 2003

"My world is crashing down to a bottomless pit. Where I continue to fall looking for the bottom only to discover there is no bottom I have to grasp some but I don't know how. I seem to fall and just continue to, I wish that I could grasp a rock or something to climb up. I'm not sure that I can, or if I know how. I just keep pushing myself back down and everyone gets mad. But I don't really know any other way. It always seems that I disappoint people <u>always</u> when someone is watching. Someone that I don't want to disappoint. I feel like if I talk to anyone they'll just laugh and not understand. I know I don't make any sense to anyone else. When I talk to people they stare as I stumble with my words. They say I'm special and all these people love me, then why do I feel so alone? I don't understand. I almost feel empty, but I know

I'm not. I'm getting myself lost again. I want to run far away and never return so I can be someone else who <u>no</u> one knows and start all over again. This way I'll already know what not to do. I could try and be someone else. Someone that makes sense, that doesn't disappoint people and this is always someone to be proud of. I'm not that person now. I know that I won't ever be. I'm just me, as sad as it is, I'm just me."

183

"Now in the bible it says that killing yourself is a sin, people say it's an easy way out, what I don't understand, is that if you do kill yourself isn't it God's will? God supposedly has a plan for everyone maybe his plan was to have some persons kill themselves? Maybe that was their destiny. Also, I guess killing yourself could be the easy way out, but it takes a lot of courage to do it, but then again it's extremely selfish. The whole concept is confusing!"

Journal entry, 2004 (age 16)

"This is me...on the verge of self loath and pity. What you don't see is the costume that I'm wearing and the mirror that I'm looking at. Sure people say "Oh you look so pretty" but I see is a big fat ugly hippo- you see all the stages that I begin to break down in? ....I hate my hair, my nose, my eyes, my arms – my mind- Me. ..I don't like what I am and if I try to change I fail! It seems that I'm good at that. I hurt more than I love but I'm too much of a chicken shit to just kill myself. All I can do is think about it. Everything I'm doing is wrong and a mistake and I hate everyone. Well what to do? ...if I'm not careful I'll wind up dead, and no longer in existent but who says that will be a bad thing."

Poem following first suicide attempt

"Second Time, Second Chance"

*"Trapped in all sense of illusion, trying
to decipher what's real and what's not.
Looking at everything I do like it's one bad
movie, laughing at my insanity. Knowing
someone's playing a trick, rewinding my
life so I can only replay the bad never the
good. Making me stuck, stuck in a jar of
confusion only not knowing what I am
confused about. Hoping to figure it out.
Hoping that I'll die. Die to end the
thoughts that go through my head. Killing
me, I want to kill it before it has the
satisfaction of knowing it's made me into
what it's wanted. Insane - The only thing
is the thing that makes me insane is me.
Lost in the circle of pure hatred for myself
and what I am doing. So lost that I wish to
blame my insanity on something else,
someone anything as long as it's not the
real problem, me. If I try giving up, I'm
lost forever. If I try to rid myself of the
thing that makes me insane, I'm lost
forever. It seems there's no way out.
Either way I'm dead, lost forever. Trapped
there – being dead doesn't seem that bad
after a while, because sooner or later that
jar starts to suffocate you and you die a
slow, lonely, painful death. Lost in
confusion, trapped with insanity and
befriending the thing most people dread,
Death-"*

185

Letter to her friends after her first suicide attempt, June 2004.

"Where do I begin? To start I want to apologize for the way I am. Things this past year have changed immensely and in so many ways I am sorry but in other ways I'm not. I am not writing this letter for you to feel sorry for me I am writing it for you all to understand what has happened this year. I care about all of you whether you choose to believe it or not is your choice.

Things are supposed to change, that's a way of life. I guess some come to terms with it better than others. There have been obstacles places before all of us and no one has room to judge who is worse. Yes, I am aware of how distant I have been and how a lot of the time rude or cruel. I apologize for this; things in my life have come to a head. I have come in contact with things that I can't even imagine to explain nor at this point do I really want to and I am sorry that, that sounds mean but some things are better left alone.

I know we have all faced decisions this past year that will either bless us or haunt us. I know that I'm not the same person that all of you once knew and I know that you will want the old Laura back, but that's not possible I have faced too many things and attempted come to terms with too many things. I am a different person

186

now, and I'm not sure if I can bring the old me back. I take that back. I do know, I cannot bring her back.

I'm sure all of you are aware of my "depression" and what I do to myself to relieve stress. Whether you can understand why I do it or not, I'm not sure. Yes, I am a cutter. That's what I have done to myself since age 10, that's all I know. I can't explain how it helps but for me it does. My "depression" over the years hasn't gotten better as much as I wish that it has, it hasn't. It's gotten worse and worse. I am now almost 17 and I have officially hit "rock bottom". I have found myself hopeless, lost and confused. So lost in this confusion that I attempted to take my own life, almost a month ago.

I try to tell myself that I am fine, and that I am strong, but I'm neither of those things. I am so lost and so weak that things didn't seem worth it to me. I cannot say that at this point I'm not lost or weak because I am still both. I'm still trying with all of my heart to find what I am looking for and truly make myself happy. I have yet to find it. It makes me so sad to see what I have done to the people around me and that pushes me even further down.

I am asking for all of you to forgive me for any pain I have ever caused you. I am begging you to forgive my actions, not forget but forgive. I am also begging you to not ask for the old Laura back because she is lost forever and I'm still trying to find my place, still trying to find who I really am. In these attempts I know I am going to fail and I have to keep trying and trying to find who I really am. Because I've lost all sense of being, all sense of living. I have lost what is important to me. I don't know these things anymore. I am asking you to be patient....please know that I care. And I am so, so sorry for any hurt that I have caused you. Please understand that I am so lost that I don't know where to go anymore. Please forgive me...."

Her fiction story: "Kirsten's Story", 2004

"Stop thinking...just stop...Oh please...just this once let me sleep without thought without effort....without dreams just sound sleep. It had been nearly 2 weeks of the same episode before bed....the same dread of not being able to shut down....the same hope for a dreamless night. She looked at the clock, it now read 3:37am. 3:37 she thought, if I could fall asleep right now...right now...she pulled the blanket over her head darkening an already dark room. How could it be..how could her brain not be tired...her body was. Her muscles ached from the tips of her toes to the last wrinkle in her forehead. Take sleeping pills her boss said...ha...as if I haven't thought of that, they aren't working. She closed her eyes and rocked back and forth, the intention of becoming

*invisible grew. What's wrong, she thought.
What is it? Me, me and everything that I
am. I can't be here, the air is suffocating.
I can't breathe. My head , it's racing,
please stop. ..... She was searching her
memories for moments of the past that
would comfort her, take her away from the
present. She walked across time and
entered a field of broken shame. Her
memories serving her unwanted guilt. This
wasn't the escape she'd hoped for...that
calmed her heart and pushed her to love
the person she was....Like venom from a
snake it ran through her blood, the poison
that killed every feeling of good, it was
calculated and precise, it's pain was felt
tomorrow along with the regrets of today.
She knew this and she held the antidote yet
she refused it, refused the will to
survive.....if only I was better, if only I had
been different."*

Journal entry, "Drowning", 2005

*I hate you! More than anyone can hate
anything! You're an awful person.
Serving no purpose in life. Kill yourself
before you continue to spread you disease
any farther. What the hell is wrong with
you? How could you be so stupid! You
want to be all grown up but you don't act
it. You're repulsive you make me sick and
I hate you to the point of explosion. You're
a waste of air a waste of time die! I hate
you I hate you I hate you I hate you I hate*

189

you I hate you I hate you I hate you I hate
you I hate you I hate you I hate you I hate
you I hate you I hate you DIE!"

Journal entry, 2006

"Like graffiti painted I can't erase it.
Mind racing and forming spite broken
promises broken understanding Beauty
shattered and rejection patterned secrets
whispered thru the night side scape to the
wall

"I weep wicked thought taunting my
head a piece of passion sipped thru words
shattered emotions said with silence given
and regret an irreversible discretion
plastered with my digestion broken torn
repent recant among us the empty the
hopeful and the shallow minded
misrepresentation against the wrong
message

"Hammered and drunk with piss hatred
taking over emptiness sinking in pity taken
up you forcing you to a pitiful soul- barren
closing all you can"

"And I'm reminded of how lonely I am.
It plays in my head what's wrong with me.
I refuse to accept an answer that there's
nothing. It's time I got locked in my head
and remained so until I'm satisfied with
myself. Distractions are annoying –
connections are incomplete- I wish I were

a machine and had no feelings to feel and no emotion to show. The sun is out and I've locked the door. Windows open and I'm begging for more. Awful feeling of inferiority. It's sinking in. I'm hungry but I shouldn't eat. I need water, that's all I'll drink. I'm lonely yet I can't handle being around. Why do I think?

'I SUCK- CRAZY times 3"

"I was so angry, Angry at everyone- I hated everything. Suppressed it for so long. And coped. Then it happened again. Because I let it. It destroyed me, or who I was going to be. I saw it as something it wasn't; Instead of what it really was. I turned angry all over again. But no one could ever know. No one ever did."

"Maybe I am crazy But still I think I'd rather be crazy in search of who I am and the discovery of who I want to be then sane and stuck in life instead of living. After all, what is life without growth, what is benefitting from standing still.

Sooner or later your mind will go lazy shut off and refuse to subconsciously move. If I reach that point, I'm already half way dead. Maybe feeling sane is me feeling dead."

"I have this gut feeling fear telling me that I can't. I'm scared to death of failing so much so at times I don't want to try."

*"It's starting to get to the point of
nerves that makes me want to throw up."*

*"I feel like something you purchase at
the dollar store it looks nice but it's ready
to fall apart as soon as the wind blows."*

*"When will I feel like I'm not alone?
God, I'm tearing down, beginning to self
destruct. Why am I listening why do I
care I don't want to be known, I don't want
to be seen, make me invisible*

*"Please don't ask me any questions don't
look at me with concern don't care, just
don't – it makes no difference I'm failing –
god I don't want to be, I just don't want to
be. You continue to spread you disease
any farther. What the hell is wrong with
you? How could you be <u>so</u> stupid!*

Final journal entry, February 2007

*"I write it down to force me to
remember and refuse me to forget. The
good, the bad, and all in betweens... who
is it I was, am, becoming and the wanted to
be. I emerge from my surroundings with
no clear picture to see. Eyes have been
closed and lost in memory of what been.
Behold the future is coming and will
continue until its past only to look back
and forgive your failure to forget. Can't
you realize what you've written now will
be translated and cut to a puzzle....Broken
bits of memory shoved into place and*

pieces missing because they've been miss-
placed. You wish to inspire...but haven't
yet found its definition, you wish to be but
have yet found its worth. For new wishes
are empty and dreams untrue.

Step aside from your misguided and self-
tortured mind. Breath-Tomorrow will be
different, the past will remain the
same...and today will speak to you in
present and past tense...and it'll be clear
why you came...."

Authors Note: Collateral Damage: I didn't know Laura, but I came to know many of the people who were damaged by her decision that night. Years into treating him, I found out that a service member who had returned from Iraq deployment had been her old boyfriend. He was troubled by things he encountered in the war, and returned with PTSD. Shortly after returning, Laura suicided. He blamed himself for not contacting her sooner. This young man now had not only to heal from the effects of what he saw during the Iraq deployment that followed 911, he now had to deal with added guilt for leaving her, wondering if he hadn't left, if he had been here, if he could have saved her. It turned out I also treated a number of her family members for depression. One went back to school to become a therapist. I attended a fund-raising event put together by her former dance associates, in her name, to raise funds for suicide prevention services. In all of these situations, the ghost left by the emptiness of her absence was always palpable.

Nancy; suicide interrupted.

In 2012, Nancy's son was murdered. He was at his girlfriend's home when her abusive ex-boyfriend came over. There was an altercation. He stepped in front of the girlfriend to protect her when the boyfriend attacked her and was stabbed once in the heart and died.

Nancy had a terrible time dealing with the death of her son. She lapsed into a severe depression and eventually had to be hospitalized for suicidal ideation. While she was hospitalized, her husband came to the hospital and decided that this was a good time to tell her he had been involved with another woman, and no longer wanted to stay married to her. He told her that when she came out of the hospital, she needed to go somewhere else and not to her home because he was moving his girlfriend in and moving her stuff out. As expected, this caused a further blow, and her recovery from this was long and complicated. Nancy went from couch surfing with various relatives to staying at a homeless shelter that provided mental health treatment. The temporary housing and therapy she received was extremely important in helping her recovery. Nancy also worked in a hospital with a devoted group of co-workers who never gave up on her, nor did I. Nancy's co-workers would contact me when they realized she was becoming more depressed and suicidal again. This happened almost yearly for a number of years after her son's murder.

Nancy was one of the few patients who had my direct cell phone number, as I told her I was committed to her surviving this. Along with this team which included her other two sons and her relatives, Nancy gradually got a little better every year. She was able to keep working for a few years and we were able to keep her in treatment and alive. One difference between Nancy and Laura was this; Nancy never hid when she felt suicidal. She knew that she had a committed group of people she could get help from when she needed it, and Nancy never kept it a secret when she felt suicidal. Nancy continues to experience periods of recurrent severe depression, but over the years, she's developed a reliable support system and much better coping skills, and her prognosis is excellent.

Gabrial* (pseudonym); suicide interrupted.

Gabrial was a wonderful family man, who was very concerned about substance issues because in his youth, he had a period where he had abused drugs. Now he was middle aged and had a disabling medical condition that resulted in chronic pain. Chronic Pain is a condition where your nervous system is frequently on edge, it's constantly sending "alarm" signals to the brain. Those alarm signals make you want to flee, and the pain creates constant discomfort and anxiety. The brain and body being in a state of constant discomfort becomes overwhelming. So he lives in a constant state of either anxiety or pain and at certain times it becomes so overwhelming he becomes suicidal. Once during one of these periods, when I knew he was at a crisis point, I called him. He stated that he had just gotten done taping up all the openings in the garage and was preparing to suicide. I had him hospitalized and following that I transferred his care to a psychiatrist who also specialized in pain management. Since that, he has returned to see me, and we've been able to achieve a better balance with his medical, pain, and psychiatric issues better controlled with a team of providers.

Cindy* (pseudonym); suicide plan with intervention.

I will use the acronym of Cindy to share a story of unsuccessful treatment of a bipolar female. She denied she was abusing alcohol but was. She was having marital problems and was in the process of divorcing, but would not take bipolar medications because of concern about weight gain. When she let me know she wanted to kill herself and then wouldn't answer her phone or return my calls, I sent the police to her home to do a wellness check. She felt angry and embarrassed by this, she was angry at me for taking her cry for help seriously. Her follow-up was sketchy and therapy – something she obviously needed- was not on her list. She didn't return to see me but occasionally would reach out to ask about weight loss medications. Her choices (substance abuse, failing to get needed help, DUI, DCFS involvement) will not help her learn to cope better or make better life choices. She's not dealing with this well. She is at very high risk of suicide with the risk factors of substance abuse, loss, refusal to take needed medication, and a loss of her usual support system due to divorcing. She is no longer in treatment with me.

Jimmy* (pseudonym); suicide completed.

Jimmy was one of the funniest, most charming young men I'd ever met. I saw him about 8 times over the course of a year and a half. As charming as he was, he was well loved by family as well. I often saw him shortly after he would be released from rehab for substance abuse, feeling optimistic about his life and complaining about "anxiety." "Anxiety" is the most common complaint of those recovering from addiction. It's kind of like the crazy rumbling in your stomach the next day after you've eaten a giant meal, it feels like hunger but you know you've eaten and it's not really hunger - except this sensation is far worse and far more uncomfortable. There's no good way to describe it other than calling it withdrawal, but it's incessant, and very little relieves the discomfort which is why so many people relapse. Addicts often die during a relapse because they might consume the amount of drugs or alcohol they previously used and when you've abstinent, that's enough to overdose. However, this isn't what happened with Jimmy.

Jimmy complained about anxiety, but also complained about how the medications that helped control it made him feel so he'd stop taking them. On one occasion, we talked about this, and Jimmy promised he'd stay on his meds this time. As usual, he would miss his follow up appointment, only on the last occasion, it was the Coroner who called me.

Jimmy was dead. He had had a fight with his girlfriend, and left his home with all his prescription medications. He took all of these, along with every illegal drug he could find, then drank a fifth of hard liquor and laid down on the railroad tracks to die.

There was no way he wasn't going to complete this suicide, he thought of every substance and method he could. This was Jimmy's first and last suicide attempt. This had never occurred with him before. I don't believe he exhibited any of the warning signs.

Jonathan* (pseudonym); suicide completed.

Jonathan was an otherwise healthy man admitted to the Geriatric Psychiatry unit where I worked when I first practiced. Jonathan was depressed and suicidal when he was admitted to the unit. He seemed to have a robust response to his medication, and inpatient hospital stays were much longer in the 1980s, so he was on the unit almost a month. This was enough time to convince the medical staff that he truly was recovered from his depression. There were absolutely no signs otherwise, not a hint. But Jonathan, on the day he was discharged, drove himself to the bridge over the Chicago Kennedy Expressway, and promptly jumped off the bridge onto the highway. Jonathan had been an accomplished professor and a winner of a Nobel prize. He knew he was developing Alzheimer's disease. He explained to me how difficult it was for him to ask for help.

It is often said among psychiatric professionals that the period where recovery starts to occur can be the most dangerous. What looks like recovery can be a dangerous combination of severe depression, and the decision to carry it out, and the relief this can bring to some. When someone is in the throes of severe depression, they can be too lethargic to plan and execute something as terrible as a successful suicide. Sometimes, in the early recovery period, it can be dangerous because they now have the energy to carry this out, at least that is an accepted understanding of what happens. They appear happier and relieved because they've decided they don't need to struggle with survival anymore and they know when their pain will end. If this theory was true however, we would see a lot more suicides following hospital discharges, since hospital stays are shorter than they were before.

There is an increase in suicide incidence in the U.S., but it doesn't seem to be correlate to recent hospital discharges. Jonathan's story does point out that suicide isn't always preventable, and that some people are quite adept at hiding their feelings.

Jeannie; accidental suicide

Jeannie was going through the disintegration of her second marriage. This likely was precipitated by the second job she took at a bar, where she got involved with a new man with a serious drinking problem. Jeannie's new relationship was volatile with drunken fighting.

During one of these episodes, Jeannie said to all who would listen, "that's it, I'm done" and took an entire bottle of her "sleeping pills" which were actually a sedating antidepressant. Jeannie woke up the next day feeling fine. She never told anyone around her what she had done, and they had apparently also forgotten her "I'm done" words the day before.

Jeannie went out with the new boyfriend the next day and got drunk with him again. They returned home in the midst of one of their drunken arguments when Jeannie suddenly said "I can't walk anymore" and laid down on her living room floor and died from the intentional overdose she had taken the day before, now maximized in her system from the newly ingested alcohol. She accidently died a day after her unreported suicide attempt, with no intention of dying.

Excerpt from Dr. Pam Wible's book *Physician Suicide Letters*

Kaitlyn [third year medical student]

Dear Momma and Daddy,

I am so dreadfully sorry for the unimaginable pain and hurt that I have caused you by taking my life. I am sorry for hiding from you that I was so deeply sad. I am sorry for not letting you know that I felt like I simply no longer wanted to live my life. I am sorry that I did not let you in on my perpetual despair that I lived in.

. .. I have finally decided that I'd rather just not exist. I have found myself happy on occasion, and I have had many pleasurable things in my life, but mostly I feel overwhelmingly sad and exhausted

*from the weight of it. I would just rather
not endure it any longer. I would have
died years ago, but I couldn't bring myself
to cause you such sadness and heartache.
I still can't bear to think of the hurt this
brings you, but I just can't go on.*

*. . . I know you may not understand why I
didn't seek help. I don't know if I can
really explain why. I just want you to
know that I may be incomprehensible and
you may be angry with me, but I am not
angry, and while it eludes me why I was
destined to live the way I've lived and to
feel the way I've felt, this choice
makes sense to me.*

-Kaitlyn [daughter]

Conclusion

There are many issues and reasons people choose to end their lives. There are many situations where suicide is preventable, but studying the topic also makes it clear that unbearable pain of a physical or psychological nature will continue to cause humans to make the choice to end their lives. Many suicides may be preventable, and attempts to educate the public and professionals have demonstrated improvements and reductions of incidences. When cries for help are taken seriously and people are engaged with others concerned about them getting help, the results are encouraging.

If nothing else is accomplished, I hope this book opens up the idea that it is something we all need to get comfortable talking about. Taking suicide out of the shadows of shame, can only help those who suffer from this kind of loss or pain. We all need to get better at connecting with and helping our brothers and neighbors. I sincerely hope this book will help accomplish this.

Acknowledgements

I would personally like to acknowledge my wonderful husband Rich, and my family, especially Corey, Vickie, Ilene and Shelley in supporting me and being there through all of life's challenging journeys, and for all the sacrifices you've all made for me, and all the times you've propped me up when I was down. I truly appreciate it. I've made it trying at times to stick by me, thank you for staying. I want to thank my parents for getting me the help I needed, and never giving up on me.

Thanks again to Dr. Robert Traisman for being the little boy who saved my starfish, and showed me sometimes it's ok to break the rules to save a soul. You saved my life. I hope you knew that.

Thanks to JB, JC, lowly fella, NL, and many others who have given me the honor of being my starfish.

Thanks to Dr. Ramesh Vemuri at Mathers Clinic for providing work I could truly love and an environment that supported my creativity.

Thank you to all those who've contributed in so many ways to this book, including Laura's family, Kotch, and Tony, and reminding me how important it was to you for me to finish this, your words kept me on task.

Resources and References

NEED IMMEDIATE HELP?

National Suicide Prevention Lifeline
1(800)273-8255
1-800-273-TALK

Hours: 24 hours, 7 days a week
Languages: English, Spanish
Website: www.suicidepreventionlifeline.org

US Dept. of Veterans Affairs: Veterans Crisis
Call: 1-800-273-8255; Press 1
Text 838255
VeteransCrisisLine.net

DCoE Outreach Center: 1-800-273-8255

Marines: Distress Line: 1-877-476-7734

Real Warriors Campaign Message Boards; visit this site to connect with other families going through what you are: www.realwarriors.net/
https://twitter.com/realwarriors

Air National Guard: Wingman project mobile app:
http://wingmanproject.org/en/page/mobile-app

204

References & Sources

1. Suicide Among Veterans and Other Americans 2001-2014, Office of Suicide Prevention. Updated August 2017 by the Office of Mental Health and Suicide Prevention, US Department of Veterans Affairs (referred to multiple times in chapter 2)

2. Curtin SC, Warner M., Geedegaard H. Increase in Suicide in the United States 1999-2014. NCHS data brief, no 241.
National Center for Health Statistics 2016

3. "Adolescent Suicide Myths in the United States" Moskos,
Achilles, and Gray. From Crisis 2004, Volume 25 (4):176-182

4. "We Need to Talk About Kids and Smartphones". Time
Magazine, Nov.6, 2017. By Markham Heid.

5. "The number of teens who are depressed is soaring- and all signs point to smartphones" by Jean Twenge. Nov. 18, 2017. Business Insider.

6. "Reducing Risk When Prescribing For Children and Adolescents" Published by PRMS, based on a seminar presentation given by Kim Masters MD, 10/2015

7.   Dr. Kevin Pho M.D. from KevinMD.com excerpts reprinted with permission. co-author of the book, <u>Establishing, Managing, and Protecting Your Online Reputation: A Social Media Guide for Physicians and Medical Practices</u>

8.   Dr Pamela Wible pioneered the community-designed ideal medical clinic and blogs at <u>Ideal Medical Care</u>. She is the author of <u>Physician Suicide Letters — Answered</u> . Excerpts reprinted with permission.

9.   Plemmons G, et al "Hospitalization for suicide ideation or attempt: 2008-2015" Pediatrics 2018; DOI: 10.1542/peds.2017-2426.

10.   Robyn Symon is the filmmaker of the upcoming documentary "Do No Harm" with Dr Pamela Wible. She is a two-time Emmy Award-winner, and an accomplished writer, producer/director, and editor. Why does Japan have such a high suicide rate? By Rupert Wingfield-Hayes BBC News, Tokyo, 3 July 2015

11.   Suicide Risk Assessment Guide: http://www.mentalhealth.va.gov.docs/VAO29AssessmentGui de.pdf

13 Centers for Disease Control and Prevention
Stone D, et al "Vital Signs: Trends in state suicide
rates -- United States, 1999–2016 and circumstances
contributing to suicide -- 27 States, 2015" MMWR
Morb Mortal Wkly Rep 2018; DOI:
10.15585/mmwr.mm6722a1.

14. Bullying sources: Bullying and Suicide -
Bullying Statistics
www.bullyingstatistics.org/content/bullying-and-
suicide.html and Bullying Facts | Statistics |
antibullyinginstitute.org www.antibullyinginstitute.org

15. Chronic Traumatic Encephalopathy source:
http://www.kansascity.com/sports/nfl/article58501703
.html#st orylink=cpy

16 American Journal of Psychiatry
Source Reference: Luby J, et al "A randomized
controlled trial of parent-child psychotherapy targeting
emotiondevelopment for early childhood depression"
Am J Psychiatry 2018; DOI:
10.1176/appi.ajp.2018.18030321.

Additional Resources:

You Can NOT Be Replaced®
www.youcannotbereplaced.com/

Suicide Prevention for Gay and Lesbian Youth:
www.thetrevorproject.org/

International Association for Suicide Prevention -
Home - IASP ...
https://www.iasp.info/

American Association of Suicidology:
http://www/suicidology.org/web/guest/thinking-about-suicide

DOD/VA Suicide Outreach

Suicide Awareness Voices of Education Suicide

Prevention from the CDC

Suicide Prevention Resource Center: www.sprc.org
American Foundation for Suicide prevention:
https://afsp.org/

Dr. Kevin Pho M.D. from KevinMD.com excerpts
reprinted with permission. co-author of the book,
Establishing, Managing, and Protecting Your Online
Reputation: A Social Media Guide for Physicians and
Medical Practices

Dr *Pamela Wible pioneered the community-designed ideal medical clinic and blogs at <u>Ideal Medical Care</u>. She is the author of <u>Physician Suicide Letters — Answered</u> . Excerpts reprinted with permission.*

Robyn Symon is the filmmaker of the upcoming documentary "Do No Harm". She is a two-time Emmy Award-winner, and an accomplished writer, producer/director, and editor.

<u>Sharp Burnout Index</u> Janae Sharp is the widow of a physician who killed himself during his residency. Her site and foundation work to help prevent Suicide.

<u>Laura Twirls Foundation – Suicide Prevention</u>
<u>www.lauratwirls.com/</u>

<u>The Science of Happiness | Positive Psychology | edX</u>
<u>https://www.edx.org/course/science-happiness-uc-berkeleyx-gg101x-4</u>

<u>Kindspring.org</u>

The Family Institute At Northwestern University newsletter 8/9/2018

Recommended Reading

Dr Fred Luskin, "Forgive for Good"

Dr Susan Jeffers "Feel the Fear and Do It Anyway"

Dr Jon Kabat-Zinn "Where-ever You Go
There You Are"

Debra Burdick "Mindfulness Skills Workbook"

Louise Hays "You Can Heal Your Life"

Rhonda Fried MS,RN BCAPN"True Love; Breaking the
Cycle of Failed Relationships"

Dr Martin E.P. Seligman, "Learned Optimism"

Reivich and Shatte, "The Resilience Factor; 7 keys to
Finding Your Inner Strength and Overcoming Life's
Hurdles"

Option B; Facing Adversity, Building Resilience, and
Finding Joy by Sheryl Sandberg and Adam Grant

My Bright Shining Star; A Mother's
True Story of Brilliance, Love, and Suicide by Rhonda
Selle4rs Elkins

Feeling Good; the New Mood Therapy by David D
Burns.M.D.

Unbroken by Laura Hillibrand,

A Mother's Reckoning; Living in the Aftermath of Tragedy by Sue Klebold, the mother of one of the Columbine shooters- the bravest book I've ever read).

Recommended movies and films dealing with depression, suicide and mental health

The Perks of Being a Wallflower (book also highly recommended)

Not Alone (documentary- recommended for teens and discussions with them)

Do No Harm (documentary)

13 Reasons Why – Netflix series

Made in the USA
Columbia, SC
16 February 2021